Amazing Grace:
My Journey into God's Unmerited Favor

"For we walk by faith, not by sight."

2 Corinthians 5:7

Troy Barnes

Right side publishing

Please contact Author Troy Barnes for speaking engagements and all other permission request at tbarnes2432@gmail.com

ISBN 9780998864495
Library of Congress Control Number: 2020919215
Cover design by Tiny Rhodes /Tiny communications LLC

Edited by Elizabeth Morris

Layout by Felicia S. Cauley
Project managed by Robert A. Cauley

Right Side Publishing
P.0 Box 339
Reynoldsburg, OH 43068
www.rightsidepublishing.com

Table of Content

Introduction

Ephesians 2:8

For it is by free grace (God's unmerited favor) that
you are saved (delivered from judgment and made
partakers of Christ salvation) through [your] faith. And
this [salvation] is not of yourselves [of your own doing,
it came not through your own striving],
but it is the gift from God.

Chapter 1

The Journey Begins

Ever heard the saying, "If you want to make God laugh, tell Him your plans."? Well, this is just one way to sum up my move to California. I've had a lot of different and interesting experiences, met a lot of people, and made some new friends. There is nothing like meeting great people who also know how to have a good time and enjoy life. In all, I've had so many different confirmations that I am where I'm supposed to be, including great peace; but, as with anything, there are always challenges to overcome. Some are not out of the ordinary. That's just how it is, or how it was until I woke up on the morning of September 14, 2017. This day is always a day to remember for me every year since it's my birthday. In 2017, it was also the day my life took a shocking turn. Birthdays are usually days where you make plans to celebrate another milestone in your life either by having parties or just being with people who mean the most to you; but on this day, it was something I quite honestly never saw coming, at least not my way. I was let go from the company that I had moved to California for. I had no idea what to do or where to go, so I turned to the only place I could, God.

As I finished my work week early to take time off as a birthday present to myself, I woke up Thursday morning to a phone call that was a life-altering game changer. My job at a healthcare company was the whole reason for my move to California, and they decided that they were eliminating my position within the company effective immediately. On my birthday?!? My day off?!? Really?!? Needless to say, I was in shock and numb, as I couldn't believe it! It's a bad dream, right? Surely, they made a mistake! No, it was very real, live, and in living color; and I was right in the middle of it. I had to sit down, as I almost couldn't feel my legs. Now, it wasn't just me. Many, many others were let go as part of a huge company-wide layoff, but I sat wondering, "God, I know I'm supposed to be here. I knew it with all my heart before I left. I had one confirmation after another before everything was even approved by my (now former) employer. What's going on??? How could this happen? Could I have been wrong? Did I misread You, God?".

As I sat there speechless not knowing what to say or do in the corporate apartment I had just moved into, a fully-furnished apartment in a great location in Seal Beach; I get a text from the one person I honestly could not wrap my head around talking to at that moment, my mom. She texted me asking if I was up and able to talk so she could wish me "Happy Birthday". Oh yeah, it was my birthday; I almost forgot. My mind started to think again, "How are they going to let me go on my day off and my birthday??? REALLY!". I had no idea what I was going to say to my mom. I didn't know what to say about any of this, but I've always been big on your words have power. The Bible says in Proverbs 18:21 that "Life and death are in the power of the tongue", so I realized in the middle of all of this that the next words to come out of my mouth would set me on the course for what was to come. I had to be careful.

At that very moment, I was reminded of a minister talking about how we are the "righteousness of God", meaning we are in right standing with Him. If I faced a situation where I didn't know what to say or do, I could say this by faith; and it would cover any prayer I could have prayed. So that's what I said, "I'm the righteousness of God in Christ". After saying that a few times and about 20 minutes had passed, I finally found the courage to pick up the phone and call my mom. As I dialed, my next words were, "Jesus help me".

As my mom answered, told me "Happy Birthday", and asked what I was doing; I began to tell her what had just happened. It is a little foggy in my mind as to what she asked and how I answered at that moment. I was still in shock, but she asked a few questions and I answered. Even as she asked, she did not react to my news the way that I thought she would. She's usually the "excited" one, the one who worries about most things at first, and it takes her a while to calm down and have peace to hear from God. On this day, she was calm, very clam. As a matter of fact, I was starting to wonder what was more shocking, the news I just got about my job, or her reaction to it.

Then, she got quiet for a few seconds, and her next words were like the voice of God speaking through her. She said, "You know what? I believe you're gonna be alright. I believe God just used that job as a bridge to get you out there because He has something for you, a purpose for you. I can see you're gonna be alright, Troy. I know you're going to be alright."

"Uh, say what??," I thought as I just about pulled the phone away from my ear to look at it. I wondered, "Is this really my mom??". It was the complete opposite of what I thought she would say, but it did take a little of the shock away. I even felt like I settled down. As I think back, one of the things I always wonder is what my blood pressure was at that moment, because I really felt numb.

We talked some more, for probably the next 30 minutes or so. I don't remember what else we talked about. We probably talked about what I was going to do the rest of the day, what I was going to do next overall, or if I had plans for my birthday, etc. I remember once we finished and hung up from our conversation, I said to God, "I believe what my mom just said. You HAVE TO have a plan for me to let this happen. There's no way I came out here for nothing. As much as I love California, God, You must be up to something. Please, show me what it is."

Not only did He let it happen, over the next few months, but also He began to reveal to me that He planned it all along. While it didn't feel good at all, I knew in my heart that I had begun a real journey, a journey to really "Walk by faith and not by sight".

To tell this story moving forward, I first must go back. September 6, 2013, was my last day working for an auto-glass company in my hometown of Columbus, Ohio. I had started in 2001 as a desktop support technician in the information technology department, meaning I was loading, fixing, and supporting desktop and laptop computers. I had no prior IT experience before I started working there, and I saw it as God's hand on my life with the way that I was offered the position.

I was married at the time, and my now ex-wife and I were serving and volunteering in various parts of the church. We served primarily in youth ministry where I got my start teaching a Bible class called *Stomping Out the Darkness* or SOD for short. This was the first sign that God was leading me out of my comfort zone. I was also doing lay ministry, praying for people as they would come down to the altar after services whether it be in church on Sunday mornings or with the youth ministry on Sunday and Wednesday nights.

One time after one of the services, one of the deacons came up to me and asked, "Are you looking for a job?". He didn't know, and only my wife knew at the time that I was very much looking for a new job. I had been working at a furniture warehouse for over six years and knew both financially and personally that it was time for better opportunities.

I responded to the deacon, Yes, as a matter a fact, I am looking," almost surprised and caught off guard.

He then said, "Do you know anything about computers?".

I said, "Yeah, how to turn one on; that's probably about it."

"Well, I've been watching you, and I like your work ethic. I would like you to come to apply for a position in my department as a desktop technician at an auto-glass company. Don't worry about training. I'll have someone train and work with you. I already know I'm going to hire you; but I'll still need you to go through the process of applying, coming in for an interview, and meeting my assistant manager," he said.

I went home that night and immediately told my wife. We talked about it. We agreed that even though I had no prior IT experience, it sounded like a great opportunity and too good to pass up. I waited until the next time I saw him at church to say I was interested because I wanted to be sure I was doing the right thing, which meant that I wanted to pray on it and make sure I had the inner peace I like to have before making huge life-changing decisions.

That next Sunday, I saw him and told him I was interested in taking the position he offered. He set up an interview that very next week, and I met his assistant manager Greg. The interview went very well, but then his assistant Greg told me they had another candidate they wanted to talk to but would get back to me as soon as possible. I knew they were just following protocol, so I said, "Ok, no problem and thank you for the interview." As we got up to walk out of his office, Buzz smiled at me as if to say "Don't worry, you've already got the job." By that Wednesday night mid-week church service, he came to tell me the job was mine and when I could start as well as what he needed me to do. As soon as I did all that he asked, I happily put in my two-weeks notice at the furniture warehouse and was ready to start my new job within IT. The opportunity was really exciting for me, especially since I had been working in a warehouse for over 6 years. I still had no idea the things this would lead to and what was to come.

Within two years, I was made a lead technician. Then, I was officially promoted to a supervisor, which I was for six years until 2009 when I was offered to be promoted to an actual manager of the desktop support group. I never saw any of this coming when I started back in 2001 since I didn't even have IT experience and just about everyone that did had degrees and certifications attached to their resume. Not me, I had none of it. It was God's favor all along with my willingness to be led by Him. That's about it.

Even though professionally I seemed to be thriving, on a more personal level I did go through another unexpected turn of events.

Chapter 2

Uncertainties in Life

While working at the furniture warehouse, I met my wife. I was on a delivery truck one day. Delivering wasn't my primary job, but I would occasionally go on deliveries when we were short-handed. She worked at one of the stores for the same furniture company; and while I was on a delivery truck that day, we had to stop by the store she worked at. This was typical as the company had stores throughout the city and sometimes in-store furniture would need to be picked up and delivered to a customer on the delivery driver's route. That was the first time I saw her. I thought she was very cute, sharp, professional-looking, and very easy to talk to. I ended up going out on more delivery routes and to her store a few more times to pick up more furniture. Then one evening I was out with some co-workers and friends and saw her, so we started talking. Talking then turned into dating, which turned into getting engaged. Ultimately, we married in August 1999 all within less than a year. While everything seemed to be going fast, it was going great! We both had good jobs. She actually left the furniture company and started working as a manager for a jewelry company. We both served at our home church and were looking forward to starting a family, but we were young, in our mid to late twenties at the time. We wanted to wait, take some vacations, and just enjoy as well as get used to being married.

One day in the summer of 2003 when I came home from a long day at work, she wasn't there. I figured she was at the store or somewhere until a little later she came home and asked if we could talk. I said, "Sure," and she then told me that she wasn't happy being married and wanted out. I said, "You want out? As in a divorce?" I was completely in shock and numb, a feeling that would become all too familiar. We started arguing. I tried to plead with her that this wasn't the answer, but it just led to more verbal fighting. It was never physical, but some of our arguments were pretty bad. I never knew I could get so angry at someone because I'm a pretty laid-back person. This crushed me. "My own wife doesn't even want me enough to save our marriage?" I thought to myself. I already felt a struggle socially with meeting people, especially when it came to dating; and now, I was facing divorce.

I was so elated when we got married not only because I loved her A LOT, but also because of how good it felt for someone to love ME in that way. I always struggled with self-doubt in the areas of dating, so to think I'd found someone to do life with and would never have to look for anyone else was such a blessing. I was so hurt when she wanted a divorce; it almost made me turn on everyone including God. At that point we had been married almost four years; and while we had our issues at times during the marriage, I just saw it as normal just like any other couple. I never saw divorce as the answer. When we first got married, we both said we would never speak that word. I was very strong in my belief that no matter what the issue was, as long as we kept God first and communicated, we could work it out. We even tried counseling a few times; but after continued efforts to try and resolve things, we were both at a standstill and realized it was best to end it. Looking back on it, we got married too soon and should have taken more time to really get to know each other. You live and learn, and we were young. I moved out, leaving her our townhome along with everything in it, and I moved back in with my parents until our separation was final in August 2004. It was almost five years to the day, but it felt like only four years of our marriage had even existed.

Chapter 3

Amazing Grace

After two years of managing the group, I was once again approached by management to take on a new role. "I want you to take on being an IT asset manager" meaning I would begin to build the process for tracking the whereabouts of all IT computer equipment. I was already pretty good at keeping track of IT inventory as far as how many assets we had, needed, or assigned.

I was also good at tracking down lost assets. This goes back to even the days working at the furniture warehouse when furniture would come up missing or would be misplaced by others, and they needed someone to go on a search to find it. They always gave it to me to find because 9 times out of 10, I would. I guess I always had a gift when it came to those types of things.

At the time my director came to me about the position, I actually felt reluctant at first. Almost like, "Why would I want to do that? Is something wrong with my performance as a manager? What is IT asset management anyways? Is there real money in that? Is it even a real position?". I looked at it as a stepdown or demotion, even though my pay and benefits would be the same. I just wouldn't have anyone report to me; I would be over processes and not people. I would also move into the IT service management model for IT, which meant I would work within a team of people to help support the role.

I wasn't happy at all, but I did it only because I was too shy to say how I really felt. Looking back, it turns out that this was the start of a whole new career field for me, as now companies all over the place are looking for good asset managers to help keep track of their IT equipment. What I initially thought was a demotion, turned out to be a promotion, and God was behind the whole thing. The Bible says, "The steps of a good man are ordered by the Lord" (Psalms 37:23). This means as a child of God when you seek Him and submit to His will for your life, He will lead you into your destiny even when you don't realize it's Him doing it. At times, God was putting the right people in place and causing situations to happen that were for my good and His glory. It also means when you don't seek Him that you can still end up in your destiny if someone else was praying for you. It could be a mom, dad, your favorite auntie, a grandmother, a friend, or a total stranger. That's called Amazing Grace!

This new role of IT asset manager turned out to be very beneficial. I was able to work with other people and departments in a way I never had before. I was able to help build processes and procedures around IT asset tracking, which the company really needed. I also worked with outside vendors to order new and dispose of old equipment.

It turned out to be very fulfilling for a while; but after about 2 years, I began to feel like it wasn't enough. I wasn't satisfied even with the good money I was making or job security. I felt stagnant and downright bored at times and wanted something more. I tried looking to other departments to see if they had positions open, but there were none. Then, I started looking outside the company; but there, once again, was nothing. Then, I did something that I'm sure shocked a lot of people including myself, but I felt very strongly about it. So, I took a leap of faith.

An old, high school friend of mine approached me about getting involved in being a salesman selling life insurance. I would be working through an organization selling things like term-life insurance, whole-life insurance, and final expense, which was basically funeral and burial insurance. I decided to do it, so I put in my two-weeks with my IT job and begin to work to get my license.

After just missing the first two times, I finally passed my exam and was a licensed insurance agent. I actually started great making three sales in the first month, after that nothing; and I literally mean NOTHING! I tried everything from cold calling, to door to door, and taking the applications I received and calling over and over. I went to weekly meetings to get coaching and talked to as many people as I could until I finally wore myself out. Mentally, I just wasn't into it anymore, and I realized I was actually happier doing IT and being back in an office environment. So, I began looking for work and getting back into the IT field.

While at my previous IT job, I had met a lot of people and made a lot of contacts in the cooperate world; so there was a lot of networking going on, which was good for me because typically I'm very shy by nature. I wasn't very comfortable around people and would often look forward to an event being over, so I could go home. With business though, I found I could actually hold my own when it came to networking. All of the connections I made at my previous job all said, "Whatever you need help with or if things don't work out and you need a job, let me know; and I will help you." Well now, the time had come for me to reach out, so I did. Even though I was still somewhat reluctant because of pride, I figured that they said they would help me so why not ask for help. One to another I put the word out that I was looking for an IT job. Some tried to help and nothing happened. Others I reached out to never responded. After updating my resume, I was putting in applications left and right. I heard nothing! Then, I started working with local recruiters. At one time, I had 3 or 4 trying to help, and nothing. Meanwhile, money was starting to get extremely low. I had already gone through my savings and

401k from my IT job to pay my bills; but now, it was all running out and fast. I was too proud and shy to ask anyone for help, although a couple of people reached out to help which I greatly appreciated. At the end of the day, it wasn't enough.

Now, the next turn of events. One by one, I started losing things. First, the nice townhouse I lived at in Westerville, Ohio. I couldn't pay the rent and fell a month behind, so then came an eviction notice. I had to move. I have a friend and brother in Christ named Mark, who I had called to see if he could help me move even though I had no idea where to go or how to get there. He suggested I move in temporarily with him, his girl, and his child at that time in their house until we figured things out. On a rainy, cold Friday morning; we got a truck and moved all of my stuff out and into his place with all of my furniture going in his garage. I took over a small bedroom in their place. Mark quickly suggested it would be best for us to get a place together just me and him as he told me things were not working out with him and his girlfriend at the time; so three weeks later, we ended up moving into a brand new development on the Westside of Columbus. They were new apartments that hadn't been lived in before. We were approved and moved in a week later. I always saw this as very temporary as I really didn't want another roommate; I was into my 40's. It would just be a place to live until I could get back on my feet. Then, once I did; I'm out. I ended up staying there for three years.

The only explanation I can give for why Mark and I moved in together and why I didn't move in with any of my many other friends is that it was God's plan. He needed to work on both of us as we truly were brothers in Christ as well as friends. We met at the home church I mentioned that myself and my ex-wife went to. We were both volunteering in the same youth group. I was a lay minister and youth leader; he was a musician playing the drums for both the youth and main church services. After my divorce, we hadn't seen each other for about two years, then we reconnected after he called one day to check on me after my divorce. We started hanging out again. I invited him to start hanging with my crew made up of my group of friends from high school and various other places. My boys Mike, Dwayne, another friend named Troy, and Chris were some of them just to name a few.

I believe and know for a fact that God placed Mark and me together, so that as the Bible says in Proverbs 27:17 "Iron could sharpen iron" or "One person can sharpen another" because of how our lives were about to take a turn. Mark and I were total opposites. Mark was the total extrovert, and I was the total introvert. Mark would have partied 24/7; I just wanted to chill. Mark was always on the go; I liked to just be still. Mark was loud, and I was quiet. The one thing we had in common was a love for the things of God. I didn't realize how much of a love he had for God until we moved in together. What I also didn't realize was that he had a real gift for hearing from God. While he talked a lot, there were many times he would say something and I'd say, "Wait. What did you just say? Say that again." Mark has a prophetic gift to hear from God especially through songs of worship. You'll see what I mean later in the story.

As I'm still looking for jobs and doing the best I can to find one, nothing was happening; and I mean absolutely NOTHING. The job market felt as dry as the Arizona desert. One month went by, then two, and then three. Before I knew it, it was the middle of the summer of 2014, and I still had no job. Even Wal-Mart down the street didn't call back when I put in my application! To say I didn't think about being depressed would be a lie. My friends were all going out places, going to dinners, and having birthday parties and such. Here I was with no money except for $1 to my name because I said I would never be completely broke ever in my life. If $1 is all I had, then so be it.

Chapter 4

Faith

Even though I felt like I had nothing, I knew the one thing I was always taught even as a child was that I could rely on my faith in God and God's Word. To have that faith, you have to know what His Word says. In between looking for jobs, I began to study God's Word and listen as well as read about messages on His grace.

Grace means "Unmerited or undeserved favor". This is throughout the Bible as written in Ephesians 2:8, "For by grace are ye saved through faith; and that not of yourselves: it is a gift of God." Favor is a gift. That fact that we are the righteousness of God is a gift. You know you don't have to do anything to deserve a gift. Jesus died to give us the gift of righteousness. We could never earn our salvation; all God expects us to do is receive it freely by grace through faith. This was birthed out of the story about Abraham found in Genesis chapter 12 in the Bible.

I began to read, study, and meditate on how our relationship with God really should be instead of the way I thought it was for so many years since I was a teenager.

Like I had to earn God's favor, do all kinds of things, or God would be mad at me and not love me. Like maybe I wasn't getting a job because God was mad at me, or I had done something to fall out of favor with Him.

None of that was the case. In fact, it was the exact opposite. He calls me the "salt of the earth", "the light of the world"(Matthew 5:13-16), and "the apple of His eye"(Psalms 17:8). He calls me an "heir of the world"(Romans 4:13), "the righteousness of God"(2 Corinthians 5:21), and also says "as Jesus is so am I to this world"(1 John 4:17). I'm a royal priesthood, crowned with glory and honor (1 Peter 2:9). He also says I can call Him "Abba Father"(Galatians 4:6) which means simply "Dad". That's right. I can look at Him as simply my father because that's what He is. I meditated on these words daily, even two or three times a day if needed just so I would continue to think positively. I realized what God was doing; He was building my faith. Especially for what was to come.

One day while sitting and watching TV; Mark was getting ready to leave for work. As he walked by me, he said something very profound and prophetic just as he often did. God uses him in that way often even now and most definitely used him during the time we were roommates. All three years we were there, God was constantly using him to tell me things. I couldn't argue or disagree with it, because I felt it in my spirit too. God was just using him to confirm it. Mark said to me, "God's already got your new job for you. He just wants you to start thanking Him for it as if it's already done, so from now on do that and watch what happens." Then, he left.

Chapter 5

Believing God

It did make a lot of sense to me since the Bible says God knows our "beginning from the end" (Isaiah 46:10), and we are to "call those things that be not as though they were"(Romans 4:17), meaning as if it's already happened. So I started just thanking God for the job He has for me, thanking Him in every way. I also just began being thankful for everything going on around me. At first, it seemed weird; but after a few days, my attitude completely changed. I was no longer coming to God desperate; I was coming to Him with an attitude of gratitude. The Bible says to "give thanks for THIS is the will of God for our lives in Christ" (1 Thessalonians 5:18), so that's what I did. At the same time, I also stopped looking for a job. While most wouldn't agree with this, I believed God's Word, and His Word to me was "Stop looking. I already have your job." Two weeks later, I not only ended up with one job; but I got two! Talk about amazing grace!!

The first job I got was working at a bar in the downtown Columbus Arena District. When I got the call to come in for the interview, I thought, "Why in the world would I work in a bar? I don't believe I'm cut out for that." However, I needed to do something, so I figured why not. I went in for the interview, and the general manager met with me and told me he had two, weekend positions to fill. The first was to be a waiter, which was not gonna happen. I've never seen myself doing that. The second would be as a greeter at the door. Basically, all I would have to do is check people's IDs to make sure they were 21 and over; because at 9 p.m. on the weekends, the restaurant and bar turn into a club with a live DJ and all.

"Just check their IDs, but also I really need a presence at the door. Someone who doesn't scare people off but can defuse conflict and still hold their own."

"Really," I asked, "that's all I need to do? Just be a presence and make sure everyone is over 21?"

"Yep, that's it. Oh also, you can leave when the last person leaves after we've closed at 2 a.m. You don't have to stay and clean up."

Well, that was all I needed to hear, because I certainly didn't want to clean up after a bunch of drunk people. I like to pray before I make a decision, so I said I would go home and think about it then give him a call later in the week. He said that was fine just to let him know. I called back the next day and told him I would do it, and it turned out to be a cool experience. I knew I could do it, and my thinking was, "I'm going to ask God to use me while I do this. I'm not here to party with them. I'm here to do a job, get paid, and get out; but I want to be just as I would be greeting at church. Be nice, pleasant, and approachable; but also, let people know I'm not a pushover. I am here to work and not necessarily make friends; so if you are out of line, I will let people know." I had to several times.

Another thing I had going for me, which I didn't know would happen when I took the job, was that I had two on-duty Columbus police officers stationed there with me every weekend. One was a friend of mine from way back, so I knew everything would be fine. We got along great! I knew if something went down, they had my back. They let me know and everyone else know that they had my back too. It was a nice safety net to have.

Another cool experience with this job was all of the people that I met. A lot of them just wanted to come out, have a good time, and was no trouble at all. I welcomed people in as I checked their IDs. I said, "Welcome to Bar Lewis! How are you? Have a good evening!"

Then as they left, I would say with a smile, "Hey, thanks for coming! Have a good night!"

The looks on some people's faces were like, "Who is this guy? Why is he being so nice?"

I didn't care. I had to make this at least somewhat fun if I was going to stand here for five hours on the weekends. Before I knew it, people started coming to see *ME*. They would start talking to me, saying they just wanted to come and say "Hi" and didn't really care to come in. If they did come in, it would only be for a little while. Some of them were VERY attractive ladies, which I was always down to talk to. I can't lie about that. That helped make the night fun as well. I knew it wasn't about "hooking up" with them for me; I just wanted to do my job and go home. After all, I didn't get home most weekend nights till almost 3 a.m.

There were some other people I met who I could tell just needed to be encouraged for whatever reason. Most people go to bars and clubs to party, get drunk, see who they can hook up with, and anything else to get away from their problems. I did have a few regulars who would come, and I would stand and talk to them for a little bit while still doing my job. They ended up saying they felt better and actually thanked me for talking to them even though I was busy.

One guy, I'll never forget, said his name was Joe. He was an older guy, probably a little too old to be bar hopping around this area; since the average age of most of the people was between 20 and 40. Joe was clearly over 50 and about 6-foot maybe 230 pounds. He always dressed casual, not too dressed up but always cleaned up well. He told me he worked for the Columbus minor league baseball team there in downtown, and he just liked going out by himself and going from bar to bar and club to club for a night out on any given Friday or Saturday. He didn't bother anyone that I saw; he just liked to be out. After a few months of me working there, one Saturday night, he came up to me as usual.

"Hey Troy, how's it going bud?"

"I'm good all is well," I would respond. "How are you?"

We talked for a few minutes, but then he said something he had never said before. He confided in me and said, "I really appreciate you being nice to me. It means a lot, and I really look forward to you working on weekends. I look for you when I know you will be here. Something about you, you're just a good guy; and I appreciate you. Don't ever change."

The way he said it caught my attention because I could tell he meant it and seemed like he had something else on his mind. I thanked him and told him I appreciated his kind words, then he asked me a question.

"How do you stay so positive and upbeat? You just always seem so happy."

I immediately knew how to answer him, as I could feel the Holy Spirit start to speak through me. I responded, "Well, God has been good to me, very good to me. Nothing but the grace of God as to why I'm here. That's really all."

He responded, "I knew it! I knew and could tell you were a Christian, so am I."

I realized at that moment something I felt God say to me a while back, "Be aware of your surroundings because people are watching. More than you realize, people are checking you out, seeing how you act, and paying attention."

It didn't scare me, just made me aware to carry myself the right way always. Sometimes, you just never know who's around you. I'm not a man of many words, so I think maybe sometimes people wonder "what's up" or maybe "what's wrong with him". I usually just speak when I have to or feel led to. Because of that, it may cause people to wonder.

As for Joe, he continued to come around every week. I did that job for one year just to make some extra money since I had been without a job for so long. My last Saturday on the job, I once again saw Joe and told him it would be my last night as I was letting this job go. We talked for a little while, exchanged phone numbers, and talked about getting together sometime for lunch or whatever. That would be the last time I saw or heard from him. I did try to contact him a couple of times by sending a text to see if he had time to meet and catch up maybe at one of the spots downtown, but he never answered. To this day, I haven't heard from him, but I do think about him now and then. Even as I write this, I am hoping he is ok.

The second job I got in the same week as the bar job was at a corporation in a suburb called Marysville, Ohio. One morning, I woke up and had a voicemail from one of the recruiters who was trying to help me find full-time work. He said, "Troy, call me right away. I have an IT Asset Management position here that I think is perfect for you." I called. He went over the position to ask my interest, and I said, "Yes, I'm interested." He said that they were looking for someone immediately, to which I said, "Well, I need something immediately, so please proceed."

He called me back 10 minutes later to say that they wanted to interview me that day. I went in for the 3:00 p.m. interview which lasted an hour. By the time I left at 4 p.m., stopped at the store, and pulled up at home; I received a call that I got the job. I started in around ten days. I sat there almost in shock. Two jobs in one week after having nothing for six months! God is so very good, but it took faith in Him for sure.

The position was temporary one only supposed to be for one month but got extended to just over two months before I was let go. My manager there was doing everything he could to keep and hire me full-time, as he loved what I brought to the table. We worked really well together, but they said because of finances they couldn't bring me on full-time. They used a 3rd party company called Xerox to handle their IT asset management and had basically brought me in to help with a project they were finishing. I had high hopes because I loved working there, and the people were extremely nice and friendly. This may be an understatement actually. People were so nice that one day a few people that noticed I was new there and that I had never met before just randomly came up to me as I was getting a snack from the café and started talking to me. Then, they invited me to lunch that same day. This happened about three different times while I was there. Like I said before, it reminded me to be aware of my surroundings because people were watching. It was very humbling, and I always credit it to more of God's grace and His unmerited, undeserved favor!!

I was let go of my IT asset management position just before the week of Thanksgiving that year in 2014. I was mad, frustrated, and downright beside myself not only because of losing the job; but also one morning that same week, I woke up to something that almost shook me to my core. I was still making payments on a car which was a very nice one that I had gotten a few years prior. I loved that car and probably paid too much for it, but I didn't care. It was by far the nicest car I ever had, and I took care of it like it was my baby. Because of not having a job for six months, I was struggling to keep up the payments. I did everything I could to negotiate with the bank to let me keep the car and to keep it from it being repoed, and it almost worked. I wasn't making a lot of money between the two jobs; but I was doing the best I could with what I had, even if it meant making half a car payment just to give them something and show that I was still committed. I had faith that God would get me thru and wouldn't let me lose this car.

I woke up on the Monday morning of my last week of work and looked out of my bedroom window to see what the weather was like. Maybe it was raining, snowing, or whatever; I mean it is Ohio. I noticed my car that was parked right by my window, as my friend Mark and I lived in an apartment complex where I could see all of the cars. To my shock, the space where my car was, well, it was empty! I stood there for a few minutes as if it was a dream and maybe I wasn't seeing what I'm seeing. It was no dream, and I was not seeing what I needed to see, which was my car. I was crushed, and I actually called off work that day, as I just felt sick. I wasn't really sick; but with the thoughts of what happened, I had no focus for work. I asked my roommate Mark if I could use his car for the rest of the week since, oh, by the way, I need to mention, he was let go from his job on the very first day of my new job in Marysville. How crazy is that?!?

I finished out the week before Thanksgiving not feeling very thankful with no car and no full-time job. I did still have my weekend job being a bouncer at the bar; but outside of that, I felt pretty lifeless. To make things even more challenging, next came the holidays, for which to be honest I was not looking forward to at all.

As the holidays of 2014 were approaching, I was doing everything I could do to stay in God's Word, keep a positive attitude, and look for full-time employment along with working my weekend job at the bar which helped quite a bit. It gave me something to look forward to on the weekends in terms of meeting new people and just making friends without spending money but instead making it. I had a gym membership; so I started working out more, even if it meant working out almost 2 hours at a time just to past time and feel better. I made confessions based on God's Word, listened to several ministers I would hear almost every day, and received any word that I just knew was for me. Looking back, I realize all of this was very important in terms of building my faith especially because of what was coming later. I was basically in what college and professional ballplayers would call training camp or in ministry, spiritual boot camp.

One day, Mark sent me a worship song to listen to. He had started listening to worship songs, but this song was different. As I mentioned before, Mark had an ability to see prophetically which was nothing but a grace gift from God. He sent it to me and started explaining, "This is what it's all about. This is what we have to do." The song was called "I Surrender" by Hillsong; they are known for songs that sound as if they come directly from the throne and heart of God. They have very powerful and moving songs. When I first listened to it, I'll be honest, I didn't really feel much other than I thought it was good. Mark told me, "Keep listening to it over and over again," so I did. One night, I was listening to it before I went to bed, and it got a hold of me. It was like I could hear God saying to me, "SURRENDER ALL. JUST SURRENDER ALL TO ME!!!" I was in tears, and it actually made me more desperate for Him. I wanted to get to know Him more, not with just head knowledge and scriptures, but more intimately and deeper. It made me feel things that I wasn't used to feeling. Before I knew it, the song was tapping into feelings I didn't realize I had, spiritual feelings where I could feel Him drawing me closer to Him. The more I let my guard down and surrendered to Him; the more I felt His presence. It was tangible. I had never really experienced Him like this before. In my mind, it was a little scary and felt weird; but the more I gave in, the better I felt and the more I wanted. 1 Peter 5:6-7 says to humble ourselves in the sight of the Lord, and that He will exalt us in due time. Casting all of our cares on Him for He cares for us. It was at that moment that I truly started surrendering not just my cares about a job to Him but ALL of my cares about anything. That's just what He was waiting on because He took over from there. It was as if God said, "FINALLY, now I can go to work for you!!" That's called amazing grace.

Thanksgiving and Christmas had come and gone, and New Year's was only days away. I still didn't have full-time work; but because of the experience, I had to surrender. I decided to follow the same formula I did before getting the job months prior. I said, "I'm just gonna be thankful for the job God has given me," even though I hadn't seen it yet. I was pulling what's quoted in the Bible in the book of Romans 4:17 "calling those things that be not as though they were".

Literally the day after Christmas, I got a call from a systems recruiter named Matt who also helped me get my last job. He said that he had two jobs he wanted to run by me as they looked like ideal ones. The first was a job at a corporate office for a fast-food chain in their IT department, but not exactly doing asset management that I was experienced in. It was more helping them build and support their franchises, sending out equipment, and working with various locations in the regions that I would be assigned to help get them up and running. It was $25 an hour. The second was with a healthcare company in which I would be doing IT asset management. I was experienced in tracking their assets, but I would come in to learn a new tool they had just purchased called "asset track". This position was only... Ready for this??? $13 an hour! Guess which job I said let's go for? The first one of course!

Matt told me that we would go for the first job, but the second job was really looking for someone right away. I thought, "Well, for $13 an hour, they can keep looking," but Matt talked me into interviewing for it since they were really pushing. I said let me think about it, which really meant let me pray.

I prayed and asked God, "What should I do?"

I heard back in my heart, "Call and tell him you want no less than $15 an hour, then we can talk."

I thought, "That's not what I wanted to hear. I wanted to hear, 'Take the Wendy's job. It's more money, of course!!'"

Before I could even call him back, Matt called me again.

"Hey man, they really want to talk to you. What do you say?"

I said just what I heard in my heart, "Tell them I want no less than $15 an hour, then we can talk."

We hung up, and he called me back 5 minutes later.

He said, "They said, 'No problem'. When can you go in for the interview?"

A little surprised, I said, "OK, set it up."

I was scheduled to go in the next day to talk but made it very clear to Matt that I still would rather have the other higher-paying job and to please set that up as well if he could.

I went to the interview at the healthcare company and talked to who would be my supervisor. His name was David. I remember talking to him about the job, how great the interview was, and how nice he was as well. I remember how it really didn't feel like an interview but more like just two people talking, laughing some, and shooting the breeze. By the time it was over, I remember thinking that was the easiest interview I've ever been in. I wasn't even nervous, which was a first for me. All of that, but still in my mind, I kept thinking, "$15 an hour? That's not real money. I need more!"; but I said that I would leave it to God and if the job was mine, He would let me know.

The next day Matt had called to let me know that he had set up an interview with the first job offer, the corporate office for the fast-food chain. It would be the following day, so I went in thinking, "Yeah, this is the one! I'm going to get this job for sure!" After the interview, I honestly felt like it was one of the worst. I had a hard time understanding what the job required and had a hard time with some of the questions asked. I left feeling disappointed because all I could think about was $25 an hour versus $15 an hour. I was looking at the money and not whether I could do the job and be at my best. I was thinking that God could certainly take care of me at $25 an hour, but what God was showing me was that He could take care of me at the $15 an hour and His blessings for me were at the $15 an hour job.

I got a call from Matt that afternoon after the interview saying that the healthcare company ($15 an hour) wanted to hire me right away. I said, "Let's wait to see what happens with the other job," as I was holding out hope that they may still want me even though I knew it probably wasn't going to happen. I prayed and left it in God's hands. I said, "God, I surrender." I was thinking back to the encounter I had where I had cast all of my cares on Him. "Wherever You want me to go, I will go. I trust You no matter how I feel. It's Your call."

Chapter 6

Surrendering to God

A few days later, Matt called to tell me that the fast-food chain ($25 an hour) had turned me down. Two weeks later, it was off to the healthcare company. For $15 an hour, I went. Turns out, it pays in many ways to surrender all to Him.

On a Monday in mid- January of 2015, I started the job as a contractor working in IT asset management. It's amazing to think of now, because I had no idea what was to come. Not even a clue. I went in to learn how to utilize a new tool called "asset track", which would then be rolled out to the rest of the company to be used for all of the health plans and at all of the clinics. The IT desktop support team would use it for tracking their inventory. Turns out, it was a huge, and I mean HUGE project. I would be the subject matter expert responsible for administering, running, and training everyone on the tool; as well as working with other departments like the IT helpdesk, finance, and security on how to use the new tool. I helped write documents or standard operating procedures (SOP's as they were called) as well as various other documents surrounding the use of the tool. I also gained a whole lot of new connections and friends because of it. It forced me to come out of my comfort zone and gave me a ton of experience I didn't have before with running meetings and acting as a project manager for the entire scope.

All of this experience boded well with my bosses; so much so that by August of that same year, I was hired as a full-time employee with the company. That meant, I now got to travel, as the corporate offices for the company were in Long Beach, California. My manager named Lee as well as the rest of the asset management team was there. We would meet weekly for our all-hands team meeting by video conferencing and a lot by phone. Now that I was an official employee, Lee wanted me to start traveling to be able to meet everyone in person as well as help out with various things there in California.

Oh by the way, did I mention it's California??? That means L.A.; and that's always been a dream of mine to visit L.A., Hollywood, and all of Southern California. I had always admired it from afar. Also, since 1985, I've been a HUGE Los Angeles Lakers fan, mainly because of Magic Johnson. I would have settled for going for a vacation, but now I get to travel there with all expenses paid for! I'm working, so I get paid for that as well. Talk about blessed to be a blessing. I had to think back to how my attitude was when I interviewed for the other job opportunity and how badly I wanted that because of the money. I see that was never in God's plan for me. It was this job all along, and I couldn't be happier!

The first week in October of 2015, I made my first ever trip to Los Angeles, California. To say I was excited is a huge understatement. It's a wonder I got much sleep in the two weeks leading up to the trip from the time I booked it; however, sleep is usually never an issue for me. I can sleep through a tornado. I remember it like it was last week. I can still hear the pilot saying for that first time, "We're making our final descent into Los Angeles, California," and feeling like a kid in a candy store.

Getting off of the plane at LAX International Airport for the first time, I was trying to see anything and everything, not wanting to miss a thing. Also in case I ran into anyone famous, I certainly had my eyes wide open for that. I got my bags from the baggage claim and took the shuttle to pick up my rental car, a nice brand new Chevy Cruse fully loaded with a sunroof. It was perfect for the type of day; it was 75 degrees and not a cloud in the sky.

L.A. was looking like everything I read, watched, and heard about on TV. It made everything I went through to get to this point worth every second of it and more. A funny thing happened though on the way to my hotel reserved in downtown Long Beach, which according to my GPS was 28 miles away. I got on the infamous 405 freeway I always heard about; and while I was driving and scanning the radio to find a good R&B or Hip-Hop station to blast along the way, I had an experience where I started saying to myself, "This feels like I've been here before. It feels like home." I felt like I was supposed to be there not just for a work trip but for good. It was at that time the weirdest thing to me; but in my mind, I thought, "Nah, you're just excited to be here; don't get too caught up. It probably happens to everyone." I had that same feeling at least three or four times that week; like this was something more than a work trip. That it could be something else for me, and the feeling was kind of unexpected but I couldn't let it go.

By the time I left a week later, I ignored the feeling of belonging in California and traveled back home to Ohio, back to reality until I talked to my roommate Mark again several days later. He had been away for several days when I got home, so I didn't see him until later in the week. When I walked in from work one evening, he asked me, "How was Cali?" I started to tell him about it; but before I could even finish, he said, "Yeah, I feel like God is telling me you're going to move there; like your company is going to come to you and offer you a position to move there."

I immediately went back in my mind to the three or four times it felt like home while I was there in California, and I just laughed. What he also didn't know was that a couple of people at my company had already questioned me about what would I do if they offered to move me there. I had dismissed all of it until Mark questioned me. Then, I started to seek God on it from that day on.

For the next year, I started to see things happening within the IT department that lead me to believe what Mark said, and I felt it was coming true right before my eyes. People were moved around and had left; organizational changes were being made. I was gaining more and more experience and becoming more valuable by the week with all of the changes going on within asset management. I had made three more trips within a year to Long Beach for work projects, and I had become certified as an IT asset management professional through the International Association for IT Asset Managers. I received my first certification in September of 2016. Everything was moving right along, but still, no word that anything would be offered. However, I knew both in my heart and mind something was about to happen; I just didn't know when.

Then one random Thursday morning, I came into work and a couple of people told me that my IT Director Brandon was here in town. He was my boss's boss in Long Beach, and I was surprised! I'd never known him to travel this far east and didn't know he was coming. About twenty minutes later, he and a VP from another department in IT walked into my area to say "hi". He asked if I could go to lunch that day. IT Director Brandon, the other VP, my supervisor David, and I all went to lunch. We went just down the road to City BBQ, and little did I know that it would be the most important lunch of my life.

We sat down, started talking, and eating; we were just making small talk about the company and why they were there in town. Then, we transitioned into other parts of IT, then we got to talking about me. To steal a line from the famous TV show *The Fresh Prince of Bel-Air*, here's where everything "got flipped turned upside down". Brandon asked how I was doing, told me that he's really glad to have me on the team, and has appreciated all the great work I've done. I thanked him of course, and he asked, "So, when is your next trip out?"

"It's actually in a couple of weeks," I said, as I had just booked another trip per my manager Lee's request.

It had been approved that I could take one trip a quarter or every three months out of the year at that point. The next person to chime in was David who said, "Troy's traveling so much; it won't be long before he moves out there."

We all kind of laughed a little, except for Brandon. With a straight of face, he says, "Well, if you want to do that, I can make it happen." Mic drop. There it was, the offer Mark told me was coming. The three or four times I felt like I was home on just the first trip to California, all of the organizational changes that happened within a year, and all of the feelings I had up to that point, now they have all led to this moment. It was no time to be modest or just laugh it off as a joke because he wasn't joking. I knew it. I'll be honest; I was kind of choked up that I couldn't answer him right away. I knew I had to let him know before lunch ended that I, in fact, was interested in the offer.

We finished lunch; and as we were walking to the car, I pulled him aside and said, "Hey Brandon, about the offer to move, I am interested, very interested in that."

He said, "Ok good, well, when I get back, I'll meet with Lee; and I'm sure I'll have to meet with HR to find out what we'll need to do to make it happen. I'll be in touch."

I felt as if a huge weight had lifted off my shoulders. Actually, it had lifted off of mine and on to the shoulders of God. I could hear Him saying in my heart, "Well done. I'll take it from here."

I was excited and a little nervous at the thought of moving all the way to California but also in the awesome way everything unfolded. Up to that point, there was still a little doubt in my mind that it would actually happen; but once I passed this day with Brandon and the other VP, there was no doubt at all. It was just a matter of when.

I started to tell a few people close to me, such as my parents, family, my closest friends, as well as my current coworkers at the company. I could tell for the most part everyone was really excited and happy for me to get this opportunity, everyone except for my mom.

I knew my mom would be sad because I'm her son, but it was also because of a situation with my dad. She was having a difficult time dealing with him; because he was diagnosed with Stage 4 Parkinson's disease, which had been starting to affect his physical health in recent years. All of this after my mom lost her only sister in November of 2015. Her sister had been born mentally retarded. My mom had taken care of her for 25 years since my grandfather had passed. My grandmother was also placed in a nursing home for the last 10 years of her life. I've watched my mom rely on faith for every situation she was faced with, including a time where my parents almost divorced twice when I was between the ages of 9 and 10. So if anyone wants to know where I started to get my faith from, it started by watching her. My mom is stronger than she probably even realizes, but I truly believe God allowed me to watch her deal with things by faith so that it would prepare me for what was to come. I will always honor and credit her for where it all started with me.

Up next were the holidays, and I was grateful to be in the position I was in at this time with the opportunity of moving to California looming. I've never had this happen before, and there was finally something going on in my life where I felt like I had "made it" so to speak. It was my own success story. I had seen it all the time in sports and entertainment on TV and the internet; but now, I felt like it was personal to me because it was me.

Just before Thanksgiving, my then manager asked me if I wanted to make one more trip west before the year was out, but this time there was a catch. Instead of staying just one week, she asked if I wanted to stay for two weeks. The reason was two-fold. One, we were in the middle of a huge integration project, and the IT asset management tool we were using was the centerpiece of it. I was heavily involved and working long hours mainly because of the three-hour time difference from Ohio to California. The second reason was so that I could attend both our department holiday gathering for Christmas that year but also the big company-wide Christmas party, which was the week before Christmas. So, I got to stay for two weeks in Long Beach. Needless to say, I got pretty familiar with downtown Long Beach and the surrounding areas during this time, as I felt it was all a set up for me moving there. I enjoyed everything about it; even though I was still working late most days, I was at least with the weather in the 60's knowing it was cold with snow and in the 20's or 30's back home. Long Beach started to feel so much like home. I knew I was called to be there, and I dreaded getting back on that plane to go back to Ohio. I wanted to stay so bad, but I knew this was on God's timing and not mine. I would have to be patient. Something I'm pretty good at.

January and a new year came, and with it came one more organizational shift at work. My previous manager was moved to a different position, and I started reporting to a new manager for my position in California. It was surprising to me, as I didn't see it coming; but I started to wonder, "Uh oh. Am I going to like my new boss? Does this change things for me moving to California? After meeting him, will I even want to?" I knew this was all God's plan and because of that, nothing would stop His will for my life; so I just kept quiet and let it all play out trusting Him the whole way.

It took three weeks, but I finally was scheduled to have a one-on-one meeting with him. We had already had a couple of team meetings, and I could tell he was a nice guy and a very hands-off manager meaning he expects you to come in and do your job. If you need him, just let him know; otherwise, do what is expected of you. I liked and worked better under someone like him, as I don't like micro-managers.

We had our one-on-one meeting, which was good; then, just as we're about to end, he said he had one more question.

"I was told you were looking to relocate and move to California. Is this true?"

"Yes, it is," I answered.

"Wow, okay, well I just need to know if you're sure; because if so then I will work with HR and everyone to make it happen. I would love to have you here, as I think you can provide a lot more value to the team. So, let me work on it, and I'll get back to you in a week or so."

I said, "Okay, thank you."

Then, as we disconnected from the audio conference, I actually had to go to the bathroom; but on the inside, I was grinning ear to ear and saying, "THANK YOU JESUS!!! It's happening now!"

A week later, he called me to let me know he's working with HR to get the "ball rolling" as he put it. The next week I got a call from a guy who was an HR representative saying that he has been assigned to my case to work on the transfer from Ohio to California. Over the next few weeks, I would work with my representative, as he would work to get all of the approvals needed for the transfer. Then, finally around the first week of March on a Friday night as I'm getting ready to leave work, I get a call from HR that all approvals have been signed; and they can officially extend the offer for me to re-locate. I officially accepted, shocking I know; and I could now start planning my move. What's great about the timing of the official call and offer was that I was invited to speak to about 50-60 men at my home church that night, and now I was able to add this testimony to my speech. Talk about the amazing grace of God!

As I start planning my move, I really already had everything planned out in my mind; it was just a matter of making it happen now. I was only going to take my clothes and personal items with me since I was planning to start all over. Start a new life, a new beginning. I would leave all my furniture with my friend and roommate Mark, pack up most of my clothes and personal items into a couple of big boxes, and have the boxes sent UPS ground so that they would arrive once I was there.

I booked my flight and a temporary hotel stay with the company travel agent. I was using my mom's car, as she had two of them at one point after mine was taken; so she could now have it back. I started getting ideas on places to live and looking at new cars. Now, because this was a relocation through my company, I was approved for what's called remote assistance, which means I would get some money to help financially. Also, I was still working during this time, so I was still getting paid and felt confident I would be able to find a place and a car fairly soon. I was relying on faith in God that if this was Him; then I would surely be okay and all my needs would be met, even if it took longer than I expected. Little did I know, it would take just that.

In the meantime, I was excited to finally share with all of my family and friends that it was official, and I was moving to the west coast. What I didn't really expect was the outpouring of love, support, excitement, and just downright partying that would happen because of it. It was agreed with my company that this move would happen in exactly two months since I told them that was all I needed to make it happen but also gave me a chance to say "see ya later" (I don't like "goodbye".) to everyone I knew. I didn't know it would turn out to be such an event. People were throwing parties, taking me to dinners, having cookouts, and more all because of this move. It kind of felt like when NBA and NFL players get drafted in their respective leagues. There were phone calls, text messages, emails, Facebook posts, and Instagram posts. It was almost unbelievable, especially since I'm such a shy person by nature and really don't care for a lot of attention if any at all. In the past, the only time I really got out of my comfort zone and would throw a party was on my birthday. Outside of that, I usually just went with the flow of whatever my boys, Dwayne, Mike, or whoever in the crew as I call them, wanted to do. I was never making it about me; but during the next two months, it was a celebration. I'll admit it felt really good. For the first time in my entire life, I felt successful, like I made it. It was humbling but exciting all at the same time. Just as fast as the day the official offer came and went, so did the two months to the actual moving day.

Chapter 7

California here I come

My first day in the Long Beach office was Monday, May 1st, and my moving day was Saturday, April 29th. It was rainy, cloudy, and dreary that day, which I thought was interesting considering the sadness I kind of started feeling; and I'm sure my closest family and friends felt it also. After having dinner with my family the night before and breakfast at the airport that morning with some friends who decided to give me a send-off, I remember looking out the window as it rained thinking, "Well, this is it." All I'd ever known was Columbus, Ohio. Never thought I'd leave there. Never thought I'd be in this position, but God had other plans. My life had become surrendered to His will for my life and not my own. As I'm thinking in my mind while I'm at the airport waiting on my flight, "California? This is too good to be true, right? Am I dreaming?"; my flight was delayed two hours from leaving because of rainstorms. I had a connecting flight in Chicago. Since the flight out was delayed, my flight to L.A. from Chicago was rescheduled.

When I was supposed to get to L.A. around 3 or 4 p.m., it turned into not getting in till almost 9 p.m. that night. I'd be lying if I said I didn't get sad and shed a few tears as the plane was taking off from Columbus, especially with all the love I was shown on the way out. No doubt, I would miss my family and many friends; but by the time I finally touched down in L.A., I was pumped and ready to get the ball rolling on a new life in Cali. Little did I know what was coming down the line.

As I touched down at LAX that Saturday night around 8:30 p.m. and got my rental car to head to the hotel I would be temporarily staying at, I was already planning my next day which was to go apartment hunting. I had an appointment scheduled in Huntington Beach for one place and planned to look at a couple of others. I got some soul food for dinner from a place called Sweetie Pie's in Inglewood and just got ready for the first day in the office that Monday.

When Monday came, it was nothing too out of the ordinary, since I had already been there visiting with the team over the past year. I planned to do my work during the day and look for a place in the evenings. By the next day, Tuesday was what I call the first so-called "domino to fall" that started me on the current path that I'm on today.

We got in that morning; and an hour in, we got a company-wide email that our company's president/CEO and the CFO were let go. They were both voted out by the board of directors. They were both parts of the family for whom the company was started and named. Their father had started the company, so this caused quite a stir around the offices and the entire company, to say the least. However, there were no other changes to speak of, and we were told everything was business as usual until we heard otherwise. I remember thinking, "How crazy that this happened my first week here!" Outside of that, it was nothing more than something to talk about around the office.

My goals were still getting settled. I was just finding a place, finding a car, and enjoying this experience. I thought I had found a nice and inexpensive car during my second week there. While looking online, I found a nice sports model 2014 Chrysler 200 in great condition. It was clean, had tinted windows, and was fully loaded. I went to look at it, took it for a test drive, and actually got approved for it. I thought, "Yes! That was fast, just how I was hoping it would be!" I told the salesman that I needed a few days and would come back to make my down payment on my next payday. Then, on the very day I was coming back after work, I got a text from the salesman saying another salesman had sold it that morning without his knowledge; and it was gone. My heart sank a little, but he said I could come and pick out another one. I ended up going back to look at some others. Everything else on the lot was out of my price range, so I just went on looking at other places. At the same time, I'm making appointments to look at apartments; but because my credit score was not high enough, I'm getting one denial after another. Then, someone suggested people who rent out rooms, so I began to look at various sites like Craigslist and others to see about that. I even went to visit several; but the places I went to, they wanted $1,500 or more for one small room and in some cases tiny bedroom. I didn't feel at peace with it, so I just kept looking.

Before I knew it, one month went by, then two, and now we're into July and still nothing. Money was running out as I left the hotel I was staying in to move to cheaper ones. I really didn't have anyone to stay with, even though I had started to make a few new friends; but no way would I ask them or anyone else I barely knew if I could stay with them. Some of it was pride, yes; and some of it was just that I didn't feel comfortable with it. I also had to turn in the rental car I had, but I stayed in hotels so close to work that I was within walking distance. So, it was no problem. I could also use Uber or Lyft to get around to places outside of downtown Long Beach, which was pretty cheap to use. I just tried to keep a positive attitude and trust God that He's had this, and everything will work out. I will admit that as time went on; the more restless I got. Trying not to show my distress was hard!

Day after day, one denial after another happened when I was looking for an apartment to rent. I felt like I had to do something to keep some money and not use my whole paycheck at one time on hotel stays. One day, I went to one of the bathrooms at work and noticed there was a shower there. Then, I noticed there were two bathrooms side by side with showers in them. They were very clean bathrooms and showers too, that means more than you know to me; so I had an idea. I would stay some nights at work, then I could use the showers early in the morning before work. It ended up working with the way the offices were designed. My desk was way in the back with cubes tall enough that you couldn't see me until you came right to my desk. That was where I would sleep some nights, upright in my office chair and cube. Then, when I would have enough money, I would go back to a fairly inexpensive and clean hotel, at least inexpensive and clean for downtown Long Beach, to actually sleep in a bed and be able to relax. Still all this time, I was trusting that God had a plan and this was just part of it. I just had to be patient. By the way, I wasn't saying a word of this to anyone at the time. I just felt like I didn't know what to say. I felt like if people stepped in to make suggestions and tried to help, it would have just made things worse; and I might have started to panic. The one thing I did continue to have was peace, "a peace that surpasses all understanding," as it says in Philippians 4:7. God gave me that peace. I also spent a lot of time reading the Word of God and just listening to worship songs to calm my nerves, and it helped me to trust Him every day no matter how I felt or what was going on around me. Even though things weren't working out the way I wanted, I still trusted God that they would still work out.

Chapter 8

~

Trusting in God

Now, it's August 1st, and I'm at work when another company-wide email comes out. This time it is from our interim president/CEO stating that they are starting a new project called "Project Nickel". During this project, they will be making cutbacks with various parts of the company, and this will include "eliminating positions".

Now, a lot of people are stirred up. Directors and managers were meeting almost weekly with their employees to keep a positive attitude, answer their associates' questions, and try to keep people at peace. People were still in fear because they knew at any moment they could come into work and be told they do not have a job that day. Within a few days of the email going out, it had already started. People were being let go left and right at various offices within the company and throughout the country. There were also a lot of people who saw it coming and actually left the company before it could happen to them. Some of those were people in executive positions, who were already aware this was going to happen which is why they left. As part of the position with IT asset management, part of my responsibility was making sure laptops that anyone had after being let go were returned; and my team and I worked with the desktop support managers in each region to make sure this happened. I would then update the statuses of the equipment returned using the asset management tool we had.

This went on for a month, and we were told this would go on till the end of September. During this time while I felt bad for people losing their jobs as that is never good, I never once gave a serious thought that I would be one of them. For one, I was still at peace and still more focused on getting my own place. I just knew God had a plan, and I just had to wait it out.

September came, and I was still positive that God was going to lead me to my new apartment, house, or whatever He had for me. Philippians 4:19 says that He will supply "all my needs according to His riches and glory in Christ Jesus", and that's what I believe. I know He didn't leave me out in California to forsake me (Hebrews 13:5-6), so I'm confident everything will work out. In my mind, I thought, "It would be nice for everything to fall into place by my birthday." As I went to look around for my next hotel to stay in, I noticed an ad for a corporate apartment in Seal Beach, just outside of Long Beach. This was a fully-furnished one-bedroom apartment with 2 TVs, bath, kitchen, and dining room.

Now, these were usually extremely high-priced, but they were running a sale on this particular one. Based on the money I had at the time, I knew I could afford it for a short time; so I called, got approved, and took it. The great thing about it was, I could move in the very week of my birthday. "FINALLY!!!!" I said to myself. It was a breakthrough, even if it was a temporary one; but at least it would allow me to relax for a little while and enjoy my upcoming birthday, which I was really looking forward to. I had planned a small get-together with some new friends I'd made and a couple that I had already known coming out here. So, just as planned, I moved into the apartment that week; and I was so happy, relieved, and thankful that I was at least going to stay here. It was no different than having any other one-bedroom apartment except that everything in there I didn't have to buy. They provided a leather sofa, a matching leather chair, dining room table and chairs, a huge king-size bed, even clean towels, and some other little things. As I was only working Monday, Tuesday, and Wednesday that week, I could not wait to get the workdays over with and enjoy a long birthday weekend to relax and also be with my new L.A. crew.

The day is here, my birthday on September 14th, a Thursday. I'm happy because I'm in a place, and I'm at peace. I get up, and my plans are to workout at the nice gym they have at my apartment complex, talk to some family and maybe friends, but mostly just rest. I felt pretty tired with everything going on, and I was working a lot too with no time off other than weekends and holidays. I get up, get dressed, and am walking down to the gym when I look at my phone to see I missed a call from our IT director Brandon.

I started to ignore it thinking it was just something about work, and I was not in the mood to deal with anything work-related. "Let me have my day off!" I chuckled to myself. Then, I got a text from Brandon saying, "Hi Troy, please call me when you can, ASAP. We are having a meeting this morning, and I need you to be on it."

I'm thinking, "NOOOO!!! Why today?".

Then I go ahead and call him.

Chapter 9

~

Birthday Surprise

"Hey, Troy, I'm sorry. I know you're off today, but we're having a meeting. I need you to call into it. You don't have to come in. Just call in. I will send you the info."

I said, "OK, I will," then we hung up.

Now, you know how it is when you're on vacation. Your mind is not in work mode, at least mine isn't. Work is the last thing I wanted to do or think about at this point.

I had an hour before I had to call into the meeting, so that gave me enough time to complete my workout, good thing too! As I started to finish and started turning my mind to this meeting, I started to wonder. "What's this about? Why couldn't it wait till I got back Monday? How come my manager didn't call me to tell me about it?" Then, I thought about the people that have been let go; and I remembered talking to someone the day before at work who told me they were starting to look at where to make changes and cutbacks in IT. Then, I got nervous, downright anxious; but I still thought, "No way they are not about to let me go, not after relocating me here all the way from Ohio! Maybe my director called because they've let my manager go, and I'm going to report to someone new on Monday? Yeah, that has to be it. It can't be me!"

As the minutes drew closer, I knew something wasn't right. I got kind of scared and started praying. Then, it was time, so I picked up the phone and called in. I was connected and heard voices, then someone said, "Hello? Did someone just join?"

I said, "Yes, this is Troy."

"Hi, Troy," I heard back, "thank you for joining. OK, we have everyone, so let's get started."

The next voice I heard was my director Brandon, who sounded like he's reading from a statement. I don't remember everything word for word, but I do remember the following words went something like this. "Good morning, everyone. In August 2017, the company started a project called 'Project Nickel' to go through the company and make economic changes for the better of our company and to be in line with our core standards and values. This includes eliminating positions throughout the company. Today you were invited on this call as your position with the company has been eliminated and terminated effective today."

At this point, my mind completely blanked out as I pretty much went into shock. I remember they told us it was a "layoff" and not firing, so we would receive a packet in the mail with a letter and all of the terms and conditions of this layoff including a severance pay which we would get completing our official employment with the company in mid-November. We would also still be on the payroll until this time, so we could receive the severance pay. We would also be given instructions for how to send back any company-owned equipment we had and would also be given info to a hotline for seeking advice on everything from getting employment to building a resume to financial aid.

They also asked us to send our email address and home address for verification to make sure we got what they were sending.

The next voice I heard was a lady, probably from HR, saying, "Does anyone have any questions?" A couple did, but I certainly didn't as I could hardly talk much less put together a sentence. The call was over, and I hung up.

I remember standing there just going numb. I couldn't speak, didn't want to move, nothing. I leaned over the bar counter by the kitchen and stood there for probably ten minutes before I could move to sit down. Once I did, I remember just feeling like I was dreaming; but I wasn't.

I sat down then looked at my phone to realize it was on silent and saw my mom had texted me. She said, "Happy Birthday!! Are you up? Give me a call, so we can talk."

"OMG," I thought. "I have to tell people this. This actually happened, and I'm not dreaming! How am I going to tell anyone this, especially my mom? This is insane! Crazy! God help me!"

I waited a good fifteen minutes or so to get myself together and build up the courage to speak because I was literally in a state of shock. I knew the first words I spoke would be extremely important and probably set me on the course of destiny, so I had to be careful. Plus, Proverbs 18:21 says, "Death and life are in the power of the tongue," and I'm a huge believer in that. I had to watch what I said.

As I picked up the phone to call, I remembered listening to a minister quote 2 Corinthians 5:21 that says, "He hath made Him to be sin for us, who knew no sin, that we might be made the righteousness of God in Him." What that means is because of the blood of Jesus, we are made in right standing with God the Father because of what Jesus did for us. He took our place on the cross, so we could take His place here on earth. I heard a minister say that if we ever get in a situation where we don't know what to say or do, to just declare, "I am the righteousness of God"; so that's what I said along with "Jesus, help me!" a few times. Then, I called my mom to give her the news.

As I mentioned earlier, she had the complete opposite reaction than I thought she would and actually said these words, " You know what? I believe you're going to be alright. I believe God just used the company as a bridge to get you out there because He has something for you, a purpose for you; so I can see you're going to be alright, Troy. I know you're gonna be alright." Not what I expected but certainly what I needed to hear. It calmed me down a little and kind of started to bring me out of the shock.

I also remember talking to my younger brother Lee for a few minutes, but then no one else until later that night when I talked to my dad. Now, my dad has never really been known to give me or my brothers Godly advice. Not that his advice was ever bad, it just wasn't about praying or anything like that; but on this night when I talked to him and told him what happened and what he hadn't already heard from my mom, I heard him say these words, "Well, Troy, whatever you do, before you make any decisions, pray! You know you are welcome to come home and will always have a place here; but before you do anything, pray."

As I took the phone away from my ear to look at it as if to say, "Is this my dad talking?" in the same way I did when my mom gave her response, I knew for a fact God was speaking through both them. This was something beyond me and what I could see going on.

Looking back, it was all a "set up", all part of His plan. I didn't like going through it, and it didn't feel good at the time. Then again, who does like going through everything God takes us through? That's why it's called

FAITH! Hebrews 11:6 says that without this faith, it's impossible to please Him. So, I knew I needed to go through this in order to get to His promises for me.

After talking to my parents that night, I remembered my planned get together with some friends the very next night at a place in Culver City about 40 minutes from Long Beach. I got scared and said to myself, "No way I can see them with this news! I can't do it, so I'll have to cancel." Just before I canceled, I heard a voice in my heart say, "No, don't do that. Go anyway. Go have fun. Don't let the enemy win and steal your joy."

So, I decided not to cancel and to go on with the party. I knew God was up to something, so I figured I might as well enjoy this new place and the party Friday night. "Just take it one day at a time" is what I thought, so I did.

Friday night turned out to be an absolute blast! I can't remember laughing so hard as I did that night mostly because of my friend Derek who is an absolute clown. He would also become my roommate later.

It was a small group of about 6 or 7 of us, but we had a lot of fun. When they all got there, I went ahead and told them what happened the day before figuring I'd just get it out of the way, no sense in hiding it. They were all in shock, asking questions and all; but I told them all, "I don't know what I'm going to do, but I'm going to trust God that He has a plan. Everything will be OK. Now, let's not talk about this all night and just have some fun."

A couple of them including my friend Nikki actually said, "I think you should stay. I think there is something here for you."

I ended up spending the entire weekend with various new friends and just having a good time which was what I wanted and needed. Especially after the news Thursday, it was imperative, because it kept my mind loose and free along with allowing me to enjoy the time spent at my new spot. The only thing was I knew after that weekend, I was going to have to plan my next step. I enjoyed the weekend while it lasted.

After the birthday weekend, I had to turn my focus on what I was going to do next. Praying and listening for God's voice was key; although I'll admit, I was still in somewhat shock this was all happening. At least I was starting to move forward, and the birthday weekend helped out A LOT because I wasn't stressed out. I had a certain peace that I couldn't really explain; but looking at my money situation, I knew I couldn't stay in the corporate apartment as it was pretty expensive. I figured I'd stay there a few more days, then I'd leave and go back to staying in the least expensive hotel I could just to get by. I was expecting something or perhaps someone would come through for me, so I just had to be patient.

As you know whether staying in a corporate apartment or a hotel, it's all going to be expensive especially in California where everything is seemingly higher. A week had passed since the layoff, and I started to get restless and started looking at my money. Even though I knew I still had some money coming from the company, I had no idea how I was going to make it all work, especially now that I was unemployed.

Chapter 10

Seeking God

I started doing what I knew to do which was to pray and seek God for guidance. I read scriptures on His promises that I know and believe to be true, scriptures like Philippians 4:19, "God will supply all your needs according to His riches in glory in Christ Jesus."

Then, Proverbs 3:5-6, "Trust in the Lord with all your heart; don't depend on your own understanding, acknowledge Him in all your ways, and He will direct your paths."

Also, 1 Peter 5:6-7, "Humble yourselves therefore under the mighty hand of God, that He may exalt you in due time: casting all your care on Him for He cares for you."

These were just a few of the ones I would look at daily, sometimes 3-4 times a day just to keep my mind settled and at peace. Sometimes when you are going through something even when you know God's promises to be true and He said you will get through it, it doesn't mean you won't still have to fight off feelings of fear and doubt.

I also knew God would in no way bring me out here to leave me. I knew He was right here with me. Hebrews 13:5-6 says, "I will never leave you nor forsake you, so I can say with confidence the Lord is my helper, so I will have no fear. What can people do to me?" All of this helped me, and I hung on to these words for dear life still not knowing exactly what I should do or what my next move was.

Now, it had been over a week, and I still didn't know what to do. I knew one thing I did need to do was watch my words. I was very careful who I talked to during this time and made sure I stayed positive. Reminder, I'm a big believer in Proverbs 18:21, "Death and life are in the power of the tongue", so I wanted to make sure I only spoke either God's Word or positive sayings. If someone asked me how I was doing, I would say, "All is well." I said that a lot even when things didn't feel well; but I wasn't going by how I felt, I was going by what I knew. I knew that I was a child of God, the righteousness of God in Christ; and that HE would take care of me. This is called FAITH, and the Word also says without it, it's impossible to please Him (Hebrews 11:6).

This is just a snapshot of how I dealt with this situation. You will begin to see later how it pays off. God is so faithful.

One day, while at the public library in downtown Long Beach just reading a book, I heard the Lord say to me in my heart, "Look up homeless shelters."

At first, I tried to ignore it because I thought, "Oh, hell no! There's no way! That can't be the Lord or what I came here for."

Don't get me wrong, I've always had a heart for homeless and displaced people, as there are many of them, especially all around southern California. They also hang out in and outside of the public library in Long Beach. I certainly also got a blessing and joy from volunteering my time by serving them back in my hometown of Columbus, Ohio. Each Christmas morning, my brothers and I would volunteer at a church downtown, as they would bring the homeless in and feed them. We always ended up having a great time; and even though we would sign up for two hours of volunteering, sometimes we'd end up staying longer. I truly believe God used things like that to make us a blessing to others less fortunate; but also, it brought our family together. It also taught us that it's way better to give than to receive.

So back to what I heard the Lord say to me, I tried to ignore it; but the voice in my heart got stronger where I couldn't shake it. I ended up getting on the computer and looking up shelters in Long Beach, and the first one that popped up was the Long Beach Rescue Mission. I heard the Lord say to me, "Go there," not in a loud way, but I could hear it in my heart. I honestly said back to the Lord, "I didn't come here for that", but I heard it again, "Go."

Then my mind got in the way, and I started thinking, "Maybe this isn't God, and I'm just imagining this or having a moment." I actually called the mission, then hung up the phone when they answered; realizing I couldn't shake the feeling, I called them again. This time when someone answered, I asked them, "How does someone get into the shelter?"

They told me check-in times are Thursday thru Sunday at 4:00 p.m. if they have beds available, keyword being *if*. I hung up knowing I needed to go, but I still couldn't believe it. I ended up talking to a friend of mine named Ebony later that day. She had called to check on me because she had moved from Ohio to L.A. over a year ago to start a new life. She's also the cousin of my friend Dwayne who was part of the crew I mentioned earlier. She asked where I was. She offered to pick me up and said I could come to stay with her till things got back on track, and I thought, "YES! THANK YOU! I knew I didn't have to go stay at a shelter." She asked me to give her a day to get ready, and she would pick me up after church on Sunday.

Sunday came, and I had checked out of the hotel I was staying at. I was just hanging out in downtown Long Beach waiting for her to call. Around 2:00 p.m., Ebony called, and I said, "Hey, you on your way?" She sounded hesitant and said that she was sorry; but after thinking it over, it wouldn't be a good idea for me to stay there. We talked for a few minutes, but I told her, "No, don't worry.

I understand. It's OK. I'll be fine." On the inside though, I was crushed, to be honest. I had just checked out of the hotel, didn't have much money on me at the time, and had no idea what to do.

When we hung up, I heard in my heart, "Go to the mission." I went back to what the Lord told me at the library. I'm going to be very honest right now. I immediately felt like I was going to have a panic attack. I got nervous, shaky, and all. I couldn't believe that I was about to do this. I thought back to the last year from the time I was offered to move here for my job up to now. It's like it hit me all at once, EVERYTHING. Even the events of the last week or so, getting let go and all hit me all at once! It's hard to describe what I was feeling, but it was scary and overwhelming. I even got short of breath. I thought, "Did I make a mistake? Should I have never come here? Should I go home?"

Chapter 11

Homeless

T hen, I heard the voice say to me again, "Go! Just go to the mission."

I went and got something to eat to try and calm my nerves, and I realized a couple of hours had passed before I finally got up the courage to go. Around 4:30 that Sunday, I walked in, went up to the front desk, and asked if I could speak to someone about getting a bed for the night. They made an appointment for me to speak with Brother Ed who was an overseer there, but I had to wait another hour to talk to him. I sat in the courtyard waiting.

To say this was an eye-opening experience is an understatement. I had some experience with homeless people, from what I mentioned earlier, in my hometown on Christmas morning; but that was more from the out-side looking in. Now, I was on the inside, homeless my-self, and needing the same thing they do, a place to sleep. Being around this is probably not for everyone, and I certainly understand that. However, I know God loves them too just like all of us. I've gained a much greater appreciation looking back on it.

As I was waiting to talk to brother Ed, I could see the despair, loss of hope, and even addictions people were dealing with. Some people were walking in like zombies, some dealing with depression, and others were addicted to whatever. It was dinner time there, so that brought in more people than normal just to get something to eat.

I was in shock again that I was sitting in the middle of all of this when I heard my name called. It was Brother Ed, a tall, older black gentleman, who came out to greet me and told me to come to his office. I got up and walked in; he shut the door. I sat down, and we began to talk. He asked what I was there for; but when I went to open my mouth to speak, I couldn't talk. Next thing I knew, tears just started coming. It took me a few minutes to get myself together, but I finally got it out. I told him I moved there to California from Ohio, was let go from my job, and needed a place to stay to get back on my feet.

Now usually they don't have beds readily available; but that night, they did. He got me in. He explained to me the two different types of programs the mission offered. One was the new life program, or what was known as NLP, where a person commits to go through a year-long course in which they basically live there, get clean of whatever addictions they have had, and if successful at the end of the year, they hold a graduation ceremony for them. They hopefully get out and find housing along with a new job or career. The second option staying there was what they call a "bed guest", meaning you're on a 90-day program where you have a place to stay and eat, but you don't stay there all day. You are up by 6 a.m. every day, out at 7 a.m., and have a curfew to be back by 6 p.m. each night. Showers are between 5 p.m. and 6 p.m. daily, unless you get a late pass and get to take a late shower that night; but you have to get permission for this.

In my mind, I wasn't planning on being there long-term; actually, I'm thinking each day could be the day I get out of there. So, I became a bed guest. I moved in with the two suitcases of clothes I had which you had to keep them in a storage room on the first floor, and you could only get it at scheduled times between 6 a.m. and 7a.m., 5 p.m. and 6 p.m., or 7:30 p.m. and 8 p.m. Bedtime was at 8 p.m. for bed guests each night. Also, two other eye-popping things about staying at the mission, basically, you were in a dorm room with ten beds in each room. Just so happens that the room I was in had a center divider, so there were really twenty beds which meant TWENTY dudes that I was with. In my mind, I thought, "How in the world am I going to get any sleep or peace and quiet?"

Some nights were harder than others, but I got through it. The only thing I wasn't expecting was what it was like when it was time to take a shower. Everyone was trying to get a shower at the same time. Talk about a traffic jam! There were a bunch of naked dudes; all standing around waiting to take a shower. I had never had to do that before, but I realized this is how it must be in the military or locker rooms for sports teams. I wasn't comfortable with this at all, but it was one of those things I just had to block out of my mind and just do it while praying the whole time. To say I was out of my comfort zone would be the understatement of the year.

The first night at the mission, I go to bed; and it feels like I'm dreaming to be real honest. I can't wrap my mind around what's happening, but all I have is hope and faith that this is part of God's plan and not a huge mistake that I've made. I lay down, and the lights go out. A couple of overseers there eventually get everyone still talking and making noise to shut up. As I lay there, I start praying and saying, "God, if there's ever a time I need to hear Your voice loud and clear, it's right NOW!!! Please tell me what to do. I'll do whatever you want. I surrender all of myself to you, just please tell me what to do."

At that moment, I heard the scripture Matthew 6:33. Now I know what that says as I've read it a lot, especially in the last few years; but this time it took on new meaning for me. It plainly says, "Seek ye first the kingdom of God, and His righteousness and all these things shall be added unto you." Then I heard loud and clear in my heart these words, "You can go home if you want to; but if you will stay, I will take care of you. You're going to have to trust me." Then I heard the last part one more time, "You're going to have to trust ME."

At some point, I actually fell asleep; but I know I didn't get much sleep as it all still felt like a dream to me. Eventually, 6:00 a.m. came, and the lights kicked on. We had to get up for breakfast. Because it was my first time there at the mission, I had to get a Tuberculosis (TB) test at the multi-service center about a mile away. A van was scheduled to pick us up at 9:00 a.m. to take any first-timers there, so I sat and watched TV in the main front Foyer till then.

While at the center getting the test and then getting ready to leave, I started talking to a guy who was also there for the same thing. He then said, "Hey, what are you doing right now? Want to go get something to eat? There's this place called Beacon for Him where they serve food, and it's a good time."

I figured, "Okay, why not? I had nothing else going on," and my attitude was actually pretty down just because I couldn't understand what was going on. I went anyways.

The same van that took us to the multi-service center picked us up and dropped us off at this church. We got out of the van and walked in. I saw a sea of people everywhere. Most were sitting, some were standing, and others were walking around serving drinks and food at each table. It was kind of loud when I noticed there was a man on the stage up front talking. I couldn't tell if he was preaching or just talking trying to encourage everyone who would listen. It all just looked odd to me at first.

I've been to churches all my life, but this looked at felt different. The guy I came with told me if I went to stand in line, I could get a plate of food where they were serving in the back; so I did. While standing there in line, the man was finishing his sermon. He gave an altar call for anyone who wanted to come up and give their lives to Jesus or needed prayer.

I then heard the same voice in my heart say, "Go up there."

I hesitated at first and thought, "Why? What for?"

I had given my life to the Lord and became a born again Christian at the age of 12, so I didn't feel I needed to do it again. I heard the voice say again, "GO," so I did.

All I remember was that I kneeled, and the tears began again. I felt as if I was being cleansed from the inside out, just like a river flowing out of me so to speak. You see, I had held in some hurt and pain from my divorce from my now ex-wife that I mentioned earlier and other things for years, and I realized God was cleaning me out and getting rid of my pride as well. All so He could use me. I mean really use me for His glory now. I had served and volunteered in the past; but for what He was about to use me for next, I needed this. I also realize now He was setting me up, as all this was a set up for my purpose for being here. As I knelt crying, He was giving me my assignment, my calling of being in this place called Beacon for Him Ministries. If Had I not been obedient and went to the Long Beach Rescue Mission, I never would have known about this place. As I got up, I had never really gotten prayed for by anyone; but I went back in the line, got a plate of food, found a seat at a table, sat down, and ate. I was pretty emotional at that point, but I could just feel God's love all over the place and all over me.

It was really something special. The man on the stage was the pastor of Beacon for Him, Pastor Erby Clark, who became like a third father to me. More on that later.

As I was eating, I saw a very cute Mexican woman walking around serving drinks. It kind of made me feel a little better, as I kept watching her and started trying to figure out how I could talk to her. Yes, I still had the presence of mind to be like this even at this point, which says a lot considering how I felt. Funny, I know.

I was also still in awe of what was going on, so I ended up going back over to where I stood in a line against the wall and just watching. There was a band playing music, people talking and laughing, some people getting clothes brought out to them, and some other people seemed to be getting some counseling or prayer. Next thing I knew, the cute woman I was looking to talk to was standing right next to me against the wall.

I thought, "Thank you, Lord. You even answer my thoughts! LOL!"

So I leaned over and said, "Excuse me, but do you work here? Can you tell me what this is?"

Her name was Olivia, and she began to tell me about this ministry and how they do this every Monday. She then told me about this lady named Shannon James who runs it; and about that time, she said, "and there she is".

At this point, Shannon was walking around with an apron on just hugging everyone. Just smiling, talking, and loving on everyone she came across, a lot like Jesus would do, not turning anyone down who wanted or sought after His attention. That's the way Shannon was. She had a glow about her that stood out from everyone else. I was then told she was the president and founder of the ministry. I felt very compelled to meet her and also felt the need to want to help out and be here for anything going on. I didn't want to come in as a homeless person seeking a handout. I wanted to be one of the ones coming to help those less fortunate because I knew God. I knew He wanted to use me in that way.

After talking to Olivia, who I started becoming good friends with during this encounter and while volunteering at Beacon, I didn't see Shannon anymore; so I went looking for her. I said to myself, "I'm not leaving till I find her." I ended up back in the kitchen area and found her talking to some people. I waited till it looked like she was finished, I'm usually pretty patient, and walked right up and introduced myself. I told her my situation and asked her if I could come help out in any way that week. She said they were making sack lunches and showing a movie the next day, Tuesday, and to come back then. We chatted for a few minutes before I left, and she was just as pleasant as a human can be. I could see a call of God on her the moment I met her; and as I will get into later, I could see why God called her to be the head of this ministry called Beacon for Him.

After the encounter that first day at Beacon For Him ministries, I still had no idea what was going on. All I knew was that I felt compelled to be a part of whatever was going on there, especially since I was not a fan of staying in a homeless shelter. Something inside me woke up that day at Beacon, and the only way I can explain it would be to say the light that was Beacon was much brighter than the darkness that I felt being at the Mission. To know that I could wake up and go there to volunteer actually got me excited!

Chapter 12

Obedience

I couldn't wait to go serve, but this was way different than serving at a church that I've done most of my life. This was serving people who the general public don't want anything to do with. These are people who come from all walks of life, probably with really dark pasts, and who maybe come to L.A. thinking they are going to make it to Hollywood and become famous. Only instead, they got mixed up in a world of drugs, alcohol, sex, and more drugs. I'm talking heavy drugs, not just some Advil, Tylenol, Bayer, or even some marijuana. I'm talking more like heroin, crystal meth, and crack/cocaine. A lot of people are turned away because of fear, probably not knowing how to act or react to them; but also because it's a "bad look" to them to be associated with such people. Ignorance plays a part in it too, but I realized, I'm sure through God's eyes, that a lot of these people probably had a similar experience to mine. Losing a job and not knowing where to go or turn to next, they had to make a decision just like

I did to go to the right or the left. Follow God or the devil. Choose blessings or curses. I'm thankful I made the right choice; but between God who was already in my life, my family, and friends back home, I had a firm foundation already which helped me do that. These people may not have been that fortunate.

I also realized no one is too far off from God; all He wants them to do is turn to Him. Seek Him. He uses people like Shannon James and ministries like Beacon For Him to show God's love and grace to homeless and displaced men and women, and He meets them right where they are. Show them God's love, but you also have to have some boundaries as well. If not, you can get hustled, very stressed out, and even want to quit at times, which I've seen happen in ministry.

People volunteer their time at Beacon, and no one gets paid. The payment is in the blessings you get from serving when it's done with the right heart. I found out early on; when God tells you to do something and you are obedient, the blessings that follow will set you up with more than you have room enough to receive. It will change you from the inside out. That's for sure.

From the first week I started going to Beacon, there was a schedule of events that happened each week which I started attending. I'm a very routine person, so the following became my weekly routine:

- Monday – Mondays matter consisted of a 10:00 a.m. Bible study including breakfast and lunch feeding up to 300 people at a time, clothing give-aways, prayer, and counseling.

- Tuesday – Sack lunch and movie Tuesdays started at 10:00 a.m. also where people could come in, watch a movie while volunteers were in the back making sack lunches and feeding up to 150 people at a time.
- Wednesday – Bible studies with the pastor of the Branch Church located in Long Beach started at 10:30 a.m.
- Thursday – Food finders grocery giveaway started around 10:00 a.m. This is when a truck would drop off grocery goods, then volunteers would bag and pass out food to everyone. This fed around 50 families each week.

Other events would go on there at various times, but I knew from day one I would be involved in whatever I could be. The only downside was I had to be back at the mission between 5 p.m. and 6 p.m. each night unless I got a late pass which was rare. Showers were from 5 p.m. to 6 p.m. also each night. Dinner was served until 6:30 p.m. each night. Then, there was Chapel service each night from 6:45 p.m. to 7:30 p.m. where various pastors, churches, and speakers in L.A. county would come to give brief messages of hope and faith to everyone. Some were good, some about put me to sleep, and a few were really good that was usually when kids and teenagers were involved to come minister. They usually always come with a pure innocent heart, and it's a beautiful thing when God uses young people. You can't help but feel His presence in that. Others came with religious tradition which I was not into at all.

So for the next two months, this was my routine. In between this, I would pass the time at the public library in Long Beach usually either reading a lot or on the computer looking for jobs. I have to be completely honest, while I read and confessed God's Word a lot, my attitude was not great. I would smile and try to be brave when talking to people as if everything was alright; but on the inside, I hated the fact that I had to go back to the mission. I did end up talking to some guys there and became cool with a few of them; but deep down, I wasn't happy.

The only time I was truly happy and felt called to a purpose was when I was at Beacon. I couldn't wait to get there and serve others to take my mind off of myself and my situation, because people were going through a lot worse than me. You could see it; and in some cases, you could smell it on them.

One day while I was at Starbucks in downtown Long Beach, I was sitting and watching a minister speak on my phone when he quoted the scripture 1 Thessalonians 5:16, 17, and 18. It says, "Rejoice evermore," "Pray without ceasing," and the most important part, "In everything, give thanks; for this is the will of God in Christ Jesus concerning you." At that very moment, something else woke up on the inside of me again; and I heard God say to me, "Start being thankful. I've already got your life planned out. You are in My perfect will, so just be thankful. Everything is already done for you." Needless to say, I wasted no time and started being thankful right there. Remember the previous times back in Ohio waiting on a job to call where God had always come through? The rest of that day, week, etc. I just started thanking Him for everything I could. The Bible also says, "He inhabits the praises of His people" (Psalms 22:3), so I thanked Him. I thanked Him that I could see and thanked Him that I had good health. I thanked Him I could walk and talk. I thanked Him that I had a roof over my head and a place to sleep. Yes, even though it was the Mission, I thanked Him anyway. Even more, I thanked Him for Beacon For Him and that I met Shannon and Pastor Clark. I thanked Him that I had a place to go to serve, thanked him for what blessings were coming based on His Word, and thanked Him I had more than enough money, even if I didn't. I thanked him anyway. I also thanked Him that He would do what Philippians 4:19 says and "Supply all my needs according to His riches and glory in Christ." I thanked Him on and on and on. You can't just do this one day, for a few days, or even a few weeks, and then stop and start complaining again and expect to see God's blessings truly working in your life. You have to stay consistent. It has to become a way of life to stay in a continued state of Thanksgiving, no matter how things look or don't look. That takes faith, and faith is what pleases God (Hebrews 11:6). People who think just their works please God are sadly mistaken. Not that we shouldn't do good works; but if we think to do good works without the right heart or think that's what will get us in favor or into heaven with God, we don't understand the Word. Ephesians 2:8 says that we are saved by grace through faith and not of ourselves. It is a gift of God. Grace is a gift. You don't work for a gift; you receive it. In God, you receive it by faith. Faith is in what His son Jesus did for us. Go back to what God told me when He spoke to me that first night at the mission. Matthew 6:33 says, "Seek ye first the kingdom of God and HIS RIGHTEOUSNESS and all these things shall be added to you." Everything that was set up to happen for me was because of His goodness, not mine, and His grace, not my works. All of this became a strong revelation to me in the time I started being thankful, and it helped get me through this time frame of my life.

Next thing I knew people at the Mission were starting to see it on me, and I didn't even realize it until one day I was sitting in the courtyard before our evening Chapel service talking to one of the guys who was actually one of my roommates and going through the New Life Program. All of the sudden, he changes the subject on what we were talking about, looks at me strangely, and says, "Why are you here? You seem like you got a good mind and head on your shoulders. You don't act like the rest of the people."

At that moment, no lie, I felt God's presence come over me; and I knew this was a time for me to witness to him. I started to tell him everything that happened and led to me being there. I could see the look of shock on his face when he then asked me, "How are you getting through this?"

I then explained to him everything I just mentioned about God's grace, unmerited favor, and how much I know God loves me and has a plan already in place for me. "I'm just passing through here to get to it."

I also told him about Beacon For Him and how it's helped me cope with being there at the Mission. He was amazed, so amazed that he told me some of his past. His name was Adam and had just come out of prison, and he admired me because he was still in rehab for all the stuff from his past. If it wasn't for the Mission, he would be back in prison because he knew he was not ready to be out in the world by himself yet. But, he believed that he would get there. He then thanked me for sharing my story because it helped him. He said, "That gave me hope."

At about that time, they called us for chapel, and we went inside. For the first time, I actually felt blessed to be at the Mission and not like I was in prison myself. I knew then God had changed me from the inside out. This actually happened three more times during my time there, where someone would look at me strangely and ask me why I was there. Once I told them, they all had similar reactions. It was powerful to them. Next thing I knew, I actually made a few friends there. I was humbled that God used me in those situations.

Two months had gone by, and it was the week of Thanksgiving. I was scheduled to receive my severance pay from the company that week, so I was really looking forward to it. To my surprise, when I opened my checking account on the day that I was to receive it, there was actually more deposited than what I was told would be. I was floored, shocked but this time in a good way. I remembered the scripture Ephesians 3:20 that says He will "do exceedingly abundantly above all that we ask or think, according to the power at work within us". That power is Jesus that lives in us once we receive Him.

Then, the week just AFTER the Thanksgiving holiday, I ended up opening my checking account one morning; and yet again to my surprise, there was another deposit from the company of more money which I honestly didn't expect. I went back and looked at the paperwork they had sent me with what I would be getting in the severance thinking, "Did I misread something? Where did that come from?" Honestly, I knew exactly where it came from. GOD!!! I didn't care to read too much into it as if maybe they made a mistake, and I didn't really deserve it. I just thanked Him all the more. What it really enabled me to do was go home to see my family for Christmas and not struggle but be able to be a blessing. I couldn't thank God enough! He is so faithful even when we are not. God kept His Word, even when I didn't keep mine. What Amazing Grace!!!

As Christmas was fast approaching, I figured the week I was to go home that I would leave the Mission a few days before my trip, use some of the money to stay in a hotel, and get myself ready for the trip. Pretty hard to do that there from the Mission with their strict rules and all; so three days before the trip, I checked out. Now, I prayed first and felt very much at peace with doing so. As I said "goodbye" to some of the guys I became friends with, it was actually a little sad because they kept encouraging me and saying they were in turn praying for ME. It was quite a turnaround from the first night I was there, but I said I would pray for them also.

As I went to Beacon For Him Monday morning for the last event before Christmas, I was standing and talking to one of the volunteers when Shannon walked out of her office and came straight up to me.

"Hey, Troy," she said, "so when are you going home?"

I said, "Thursday," which was in a few days.

She then said, "Are you coming back?"

I said, "Oh yeah, I'll be back," but in my mind, I'm thinking, "I hope I'm coming back; but without a job and place to stay, I'm really not sure why I would come back."

Then again I felt in my heart that I was supposed to be here, so once again I would be acting on faith.

Shannon then said, "Well, when you do, I don't want you to go back to the Mission. I want you to stay here at Beacon. Now, I want you to pray about it, but I've already been praying and think it would be good. Let me know when you get back if you want to."

I once again almost went into shock. First, had just checked out of the Mission. Second, I thought, "Stay here? In a church?" Now the church was big enough where you could have your own room, and there were a full bathroom and shower in the back. I had never even realized anyone was really staying here full time.

A few people around us that heard her all said, "Yeah, Troy, you should do that! It would be good. They need you here."

I was still floored by all this, and it gave me a lot to think about. In my heart, I knew the moment she asked me that I was supposed to say "yes" and do it. I still waited until I got back to let her know though, as I wanted to be sure; but I heard God's voice say already, "Yes, do it."

Chapter 13

Volunteering

I came back from Ohio after Christmas and went to Beacon that week to tell Shannon that I would stay there. I stayed in a hotel for a week just to give them time to have a spot ready for me. Once I got there, I was fully committed to helping out wherever they needed help or whenever it was needed. I got to learn more about Beacon, Shannon, and just how the ministry got started.

The most fascinating thing to me was getting to know Shannon James. Here was a woman with a family, mother of 4 with a full-time job, and also running a ministry with no real experience other than she does what God tells her to do. Many on the outside may wonder, "Why Shannon?," but God gave me a couple of different revelations as to why He chose her.

First of all, she has His heart. She has her own testimony, which I will not get into, but she has the biggest heart of anyone I know. She is also one of the nicest and most giving people I know. I remember one time early on when I started volunteering, she was talking to someone and asked me to come to pray with a young man.

She commented, "This is my brother, Troy."

I said in a joking way, "Yes, can't you see we look just alike?"

But it wasn't a joking moment, and I felt God get on me for that in my heart.

He then started talking to me about Shannon one evening while at the Mission; and he said to me, "Shannon is your sister. She's family, treat her like family, like you would a real sister. Support her, pray for her, and most importantly," this was key, "do whatever she tells you to do. By doing so, you will honor me."

Man, talk about a Word from God and acting out on faith! Since up to that point, she hardly even knew me and vice versa.

From that moment on, I did just what He told me, and I did it happily. The more Shannon and I talked about things and the ministry; the more connected we became. She really started feeling like my sister, not just a sister in Christ although she was that too. I took pleasure in supporting her and doing whatever she told me to do, even checking on her from time to time to make sure she was okay. It takes a lot to run a ministry, but I was happy to do my part. All of the volunteers became a family to me, which I realized this was a total set up by God to place me within a family that would keep me grounded and in HIS will for my life and not mine.

Whether our doors to Beacon were open or not, people would also come looking for Shannon. Some even walked out angry if she wasn't there like I wasn't good enough to help them with their needs. It didn't bother me. I understood. I began to feel the same way about Shannon and love her just as they did. She has such a joy and love about her that people want to just be around her, if for no other reason than just to talk.

On another evening while still at the Mission, I heard God say to me, "Look up the definition of the word 'Beacon.'" I did, and one of the definitions was that Beacon meant, "a light, a warning, and a guide". That's what Shannon is, and that's what we all should be at Beacon For Him. We should be a light, a warning, and a guide to HIM, meaning God through His son Jesus. It's no wonder so many people love Shannon.

While I was staying at Beacon full-time, several things took place. We had to stop serving food out of our kitchen because the city's health department came in and said it wasn't up to code. While this was a huge disappointment because serving meals was a big part of the ministry, on the flip side, we started our own church on Sundays with our Pastor Clark officiating. I had not chosen a church home for myself, so I started serving the pastor here every Sunday. We also started a Wednesday night Bible study. Both of these did not draw huge crowds; because other than some coffee and donuts at times, we weren't serving the food that people were looking for.

Instead, I felt God leading us to serve more spiritual food for people's souls, which many of them desperately needed. God began to use me more on Sundays to assist Pastor Clark; I set up chairs, cleaned up, collected offerings or any donations, and even learned how to work the AV equipment for each service. One Sunday early on, the pastor asked me to give my testimony, so I did. From that day on, he had me start every service with our "scripture of the day". Instead of just picking out scripture to read then sitting down like I didn't want to be bothered, I felt God lead me to take five minutes and really teach the scriptures that He would give to me, just like I learned about the scriptures for myself. It really began to witness to people, and I could see what was happening. God was training me for a ministry of my own.

I thank Pastor Clark for hearing from God and allowing me to do it. Things like this actually helped to build my relationship with the pastor; it gave me sort of a mentor, like a 3rd father, starting with God the father, my dad back home in Ohio, and now Pastor Clark. Pastor Clark is also from Mississippi, just like my real dad; and he even reminds me of my dad in a lot of ways.

It was a total set up from God that brought us together, and he has a ton of wisdom from all his years in ministry. I actually could sit and listen to him tell stories all day; and since we weren't serving any kind of food or drink during our Wednesday evening Bible study most of the time, it would just turn into me and him talking about anything from the goodness of God, to the Bible, or maybe even the Lakers now and then, as we are both fans.

Each week was pretty much the same, although it wasn't all ministry, I did have the opportunity to go out, meet people, and make a few new friends. It was a little difficult to wrap my head around doing all of this with no job or car of my own. I often had to block out what people's perceptions might be, but I was quick to let them and even myself know at times that I'm still standing on God's Word and my faith in it.

Sometimes people would try to help and give me advice, especially in looking for jobs. I would take their advice and thank them, but something inside of me would then say, "Stop worrying about your job. I already got that, remember?"

Then I would say, "Yeah, but when?"

God told me this on three different occasions, "Stop looking. I got your job. Just be thankful."

Then, I would shut up and remember to just thank Him as I mentioned before from the scripture found in 1 Thessalonians 5:18. I continually would thank Him no matter what, even when I would get restless.

One day in March at Beacon, an evangelist couple that partners with the ministry named David and Kathy stopped by to pray at Beacon. I didn't know they were supposed to come, but I let them in and let them do their thing. I actually sat in on it. When they were finished, they were about to leave when David said, "I'm going to pray for you now," so he did. When he finished, he said, "God says He's got your job and your car. You're about to get it."

I thanked them; then they left. Just like that, I thought, "OK, I believe and totally receive that, so I'm ready. Bring it on."

That was on a Friday. The following Tuesday night, I'm sitting in the office at Beacon by myself watching the Lakers game when I get a text from someone I used to work with at my old company in downtown Long Beach. The text said to call a number and that there was a job opening that she thought I would be perfect for. I said, "OK, I will call them first thing in the morning." I immediately remembered the prayer from the previous Friday but also downplayed it a little as to not get too excited. I kept watching the game, the Lakers won; then, I went to bed and to sleep.

When I got up the next day, I had every intention of calling the number to see about the job. I called, and a recruiter answered the phone. When I told her who I was and why I was calling she said, "Oh wow! That's awesome because I have your resume here in front of me and was going to call you." Look at God! We talked for about 30 minutes, then she said she would call back later. She called back an hour later and asked if I could interview for an IT asset coordinator position with a company in Torrance. I said, "Sure," and she sent me an email with the specifics of the job and who I would be talking to and what time. It was for the next day; on a Wednesday, I had what would be my second interview. After this interview, I was then asked to have yet a 3rd interview with the same company the following week; but this time on-site so I accepted and did. Finally, I was asked for one more interview, but this time it was to go to Irvine, CA to meet with a car company where I would be working on-site as their IT Asset Coordinator. If there's no heavy traffic, Irvine is about 35 minutes away from Long Beach. I had to meet with the managers of a company there, which is where I would ultimately be working.

I didn't have a car yet, so anywhere I went outside of downtown Long Beach, I took an Uber or Lyft. When we pulled up, it was about the nicest area I think I ever seen. Irvine itself is very upscale, and you can tell right away it's pretty expensive to live there. I got out and went in for my now 4th interview for this IT asset coordinator job. By the time it was over, I just had this feeling in my heart and soul that this was it. Kind of hard to explain, but I remember asking God while saying to myself, "This is it, isn't it?" I didn't hear a response, but I just knew it.

Two days later on a Thursday morning, while at Beacon doing our grocery give-a-way, I got the call that the job was mine, and I would start Monday, April 23rd. Talk about God being faithful! I would have to say between the severance pay I got from my old company, the new job, and all the other many blessings coming my way during this time; it made the time of getting let go and staying at the Mission almost worth it because of how it changed me from the inside out. I was so happy, relieved, full of joy, etc.

Wait, there's more!

Once it was secure that I now had a job, the next domino that had to fall was that I needed transportation to get to work. Anyone that knows anything about L.A. traffic knows it's not the fastest. I always tell people to leave at least an additional 30 minutes if not an hour ahead of when you would normally plan to if you're taking the highways because sometimes you just never know. Even on weekends, it can be a lot. In my mind and heart, I knew being a child of God and remembering what He told me that first night at the Mission; I knew He would supply my needs as His Word says. It doesn't mean doubt didn't try to knock on the door of my mind. I remember in the interviews, two different times I was asked if I had a car. They asked because I had told them I moved from Ohio and was let go from my job and was still trying to get on my feet. I remembered saying without hesitation, "I'll have a car, no worries; I will get to work."

"Are you sure?" they asked.

I responded, "Yes, I'll have one and will get here, no problem."

Now at the time, my mind was saying, "Say what?!? How do you know? What if you don't?"

That was just the enemy trying to insert doubt, but I really believed what God's Word says and more importantly what He's told me all along. Even as recent as a couple of weeks before when the evangelist David prayed for me at Beacon, he said God was about to give me the job AND THE CAR! So, I rested on that.

I started to look into bus routes on how to get from Long Beach to Irvine, but then I heard God say in my heart, "I told you a car." I immediately let that go. When I told Shannon about getting the job, she even said, "You're going to have your car by the first day of work." She was determined to pray and see to it as well, even going as far as putting the word out to anyone willing to donate cars or any type of transportation. Other volunteers stepped up willing to help with either taking me to work or loaning me a car temporarily until I could get my own. I was really floored and humbled by all the support. I could feel God's presence, love, and favor in all of it; but I was also relying on another scripture as well so that I didn't get too anxious or nervous. Matthew 11:28 says, "Come unto me all who labor and are heavy laden, and I will give you rest." It also goes on to say that His yoke is easy, and His burden is light. Hebrews 4:11 also says, "Let us labor therefore to enter into the rest of God lest any man fall after the same example of unbelief." When you're in the rest of God, I can honestly say you have a peace that passes all understanding. That even while things may not look, sound, or be right around you; you can still say and even declare that "ALL IS WELL". That's what's called exercising your faith.

While studying His Word in between looking at jobs, God showed me how faith is like muscles in your body. Everyone born into this world has muscles, whether you can see them or not. The ones that go to the gym regularly make it a lifestyle of not only working out but also making sure what they put in their body feeds their muscles, and they will see results. Some are more fully developed than others, but faith works the same way. If we are constantly filling our minds with doubt, unbelief, and what can't be done; then our faith in God can't grow. When we fill ourselves with God's word, His promises, as well as an attitude of thanking Him for what He's already done even when we can't see it yet; our faith grows. We will eventually see His promises come to pass in our lives. Faith in HIM is what we have to stand on though to make this happen.

So while the first day of work is getting closer and all the offers are coming in for how I'm going to get to work, isn't it just like God to pull an end-around or a double reverse? (Those are terms used to describe plays in football usually meaning to do the unexpected.) It's down to my last Sunday before my first official day at work and still no car of my own. Although, I had one of the volunteers at Beacon set up to take me to work and pick me up afterward, as well as another volunteer that was going to loan me a car for a couple of weeks but had to get it checked out first. We had our usual church service that morning at Beacon, then afterward I had planned to go to this restaurant called The BB restaurant in downtown Long Beach; not only because they have really good food, but I've made some good friends there, one of them being the manager whose name is Rebecca. Everyone calls her "Bex" for short.

I met Rebecca for my very first time at the BB when I walked in. It was pretty crowded, and she greeted me. I told her I was from out of town, had just moved here, and was just looking to get some good breakfast food, which I love any time of the day or night. She sat me at the bar, got me my order very quickly, and even took care of the bill which surprised me a little; but I know with the favor of God, I have these types of things happen a lot. It just made an impression of how nice she was right away. The more I kept coming back and the more I got to know her, I realized everyone loves Bex! Between managing the BB and also working at L Bar at Belmont Shore on the very popular 2nd street in Long Beach, she knows A LOT of people; and everyone loves her. We instantly became good friends, and she even invited me out to meet more people to make new friends. That's just the type of kind-hearted person she is. She reminds me of my sister Shannon in that way as well. I love how God places and connects certain people in my life. He told me at the Mission, "I will add all things to you for seeking and trusting me." (Matthew 6:33)

More than the food, I was anxious to go to the BB that day to talk to Bex and tell her about my new job, as she was one of the main ones always checking on me and making sure I was okay. I couldn't wait to tell her everything! As I ordered my food and we sat and talked, she like everyone else told me how happy and proud of me she was. All of a sudden she stopped and said, "So, how are you getting to work?"

I replied, "Well, I've got someone taking me to work tomorrow, as well as picking me up. Then, also another friend of mine from Beacon is offering to loan me his car, but he has to get it checked out first. I should have it by Tuesday, so I'll get to and from work. No need to worry."

Then Bex, "Well, why don't I just loan you my car for a month or so until you're able to make some money? Then, you can buy your own. I'll maybe loan you the car until you can get your own"

As I'm once again floored and in awe of her also offering to help with the situation, she then stopped and took it a step farther than anyone else I had talked to.

"No, that's not right," she said. "Why don't I just give you my car? Yeah, that's it! I'm just gonna give it to you!"

At this point, my food comes out to me, but I can hardly eat it as I felt like something out of the twilight zone hit me. I was in shock again. In my mind, I almost said, "No, you don't have to do that;" but I knew better. This was once again God coming through faithful with His Word.

She then says, "Okay, here's what we're gonna do. I'm going to go home and talk it over with my fiancé; but don't worry, he's got a heart just like mine. He'll be fine with this. If he didn't, I wouldn't marry him," she laughed, "but I'm going to talk to him and will call you later to work out getting the car to you. Since you already have a way to work tomorrow, if I don't get it to you tonight, I'll get it to you after work tomorrow."

I managed to agree to everything, finished eating my food, and hung out with my friends there till the close of business around 3 p.m. that day; but I'll be honest, God's blessing and favor overtook me at that moment. There's another scripture in the book of Deuteronomy 28: 1-2 where it talks about "when you obey the voice of the Lord thy God that all these blessings shall come on thee and overtake thee". I thought back to the voice that told me to go to the Long Beach Rescue Mission that weekend I went and how because I obeyed, these are all the blessings coming into full manifestation now. It's still happening all because I made that one decision to obey and go. I also thought about how things might have turned out had I not obeyed and went when He told me to. To be honest, I'd probably be one of those people on the street I mentioned earlier, all because of pride. Then I thought, "This must be how a lot of people end up there because of their pride."

About 2 ½ hours after I left the BB, I was walking back to Beacon after running a couple of errands to get ready for my first day at work; when my phone started ringing, I looked down to see it was Bex. I answered, and she said, "Hey, where are you? I'm getting ready to bring you your car."

Tears started to form in my eyes, as she really just said "YOUR" car. I told her I was walking back to Beacon and almost there, so I would text her the address.

She said, "Okay, be there in 20 minutes."

I waited outside, as I was pretty excited about it all; and sure enough, twenty minutes later, she pulled up in MY car, got out, and handed me the keys.

She said, "Okay, here are the keys to your car. Now, take me back home, so I can get there please."

The funny thing was that she had to say that because I was so in awe of the moment; I wasn't even thinking about how she would get home! I thanked her for reminding me. Maybe she could see that written all over my face. We laughed about it. Then I took her home, met her fiancé, and thanked him as well. Now, I was all ready to start my first day at work and to drive my first car since moving to California. To God be ALL THE GLORY!!!

Chapter 14

God's Promises Are True

After a year and a half of staying at Beacon for Him for shelter, working at the company in Irvine, and driving the car I had been blessed with, there was another shift. The church building I had been staying in was going to have to close its doors. Bottom line is, some of the money that had been coming in to keep the doors open was not there anymore; and Shannon had to make the tough decision to close shop and move somewhere else. The ministry itself kept going just at a different location; however, it meant myself along with the three other guys that stayed there as gatekeepers would have to leave. Shannon set up housing for the other guys, but only two accepted it. Then, there was me. The funny thing was for several months I had already been feeling like it was time for me to move and find a place of my own, primarily to be a lot closer to Irvine and my current job. Technically, I was only 35 miles away from work; but in Southern California traffic and driving at times of rush hour, it meant anywhere from one to two and a half hours of travel time. After a long and busy workday, it could get to be a grind. While I was elated to be working and with the things God was doing; I was getting tired, very tired.

I had started looking at several places around the Huntington Beach area, but nothing stood out. Then, thinking back to all the other times I just prayed and left it alone to God, I stopped looking and said, "I know you have a place for me, so just lead me to it." I then recollected something I had completely forgotten about. I had seen the evangelist David a couple of months prior at Beacon for an event going on there. As he and his wife were leaving, we were talking. He all of sudden said, "Let me pray for you." He prayed. Then when finished, he said, "God's got a house for you. I see you moving into a house soon." I was floored but also remembered what my brother and roommate from Ohio Mark had told me when I went home to visit for Christmas a year prior. He said that he saw the same thing; I would be moving into a house. I just received it and trusted it would happen. I mean, God's track record has been working pretty good for me when I trust Him. Why would I ever stop now? Right?

One day while at work, my friend Derek (from my birthday party) and I were talking at lunch, as he worked for the same company in Irvine. He actually moved from Columbus, Ohio to California to start working there and had been here since 2011. It was so funny on my 2nd day on the job seeing Derek around the elevator. He had told me when we first met at Ebony's birthday party back three weeks after I had moved here in May 2017 that he worked for this car company, but I had completely forgotten until the day I saw him by the elevator. Derek and I are both from the same city in Ohio, have a lot of the same friends, have been to all the same places at the same time; and we had never met until that birthday party. We both still laugh about it to this day. While we were hanging at lunch, we were talking; and he told me he and another guy named Kiran (who I also met at Ebony's birthday party) were looking to get a place together and wanted to add a 3rd roommate. I said "Funny, I'm looking to find a place closer, especially one closer to work." Initially, I wasn't sure I wanted to do the roommate thing again because I'm more of a private person who likes to keep to myself and have my own space, but it's expensive to live here in California! If not married with two incomes, most people survive financially by having a roommate. Plus, Derek and Kiran weren't just looking for a place; they were looking for really huge places in really nice areas of Orange County. The thought was to get a nice, big place for rent while splitting three ways. That way we could afford it along with each person having enough space to live and still have his own privacy. We are three grown men, so the idea made sense. Plus, as I said, the church building for Beacon was closing their doors, so it was definitely time to make a move.

One day while going to meet a friend in Seal Beach, I ended up running into Kiran, my other future roommate. Kiran is originally from India and used to work at the same company as Derek and me, which is how he and Derek met and became friends. It was completely unexpected when we ran into each other that evening; but considering the time that we were looking to become roommates, it was good to see him. After we talked, it ended up being more confirmation for me of what was to come, as we all got along great. We would be roommates, so when I could, I joined them after work to go out looking for places to live. I was never worried about finding something because I knew it would happen at the right time. Suddenly, just as Beacon found another place for the ministry and all but closed its doors on the current building to the public and their moving process had begun, I was out with Derek and Kiran helping our friend Ebony move into her new place. Derek got a call from a realtor to let him know we had gotten approved for a huge house in Lake Forest that I hadn't even seen yet. Lake Forest is a neighboring city to Irvine, and it would only be 15-20 minutes at most to travel to work. It was a house that the two of them had went to look at without me a week or two prior. Our move-in date would be mid-June. Once again, God's Word became true, and I didn't even need to be there for the house to be found. I was moving into a house and just in time. I've moved in as I've finished writing this book.

One of the most important things I've learned when surrendering to God's will for my life, which basically means exchanging our will for His just as Jesus took on our life at the cross and gave us His to live now, is that what happens in you will always be greater than anything that happens to you. Not that you still won't have some of the "one of those days" type of things or some days won't be more challenging than others; but when you keep your mind on him, "He will keep you in perfect peace" (Isaiah 26:3). God isn't mad at us. His true nature is to bless us; and by that I mean empower us to prosper in everything our hands touch or in everything our name is associated with, I believe. The key is to surrender to His will, and I can truly testify things in my life go a lot easier and smoother when I cast my cares on Him (I Peter 5:6-7).

Also, we as believers in Christ need to understand that we have an inheritance that only comes by way of Jesus and His death on the cross. It's called the blessing of Abraham. There are various scriptures such as Genesis chapters 12 through 20 and Deuteronomy chapter 28. In the New Testament, there are Galatians chapter 3 along with Romans chapter 4. These scriptures breakdown the relationship that God had with Abraham after the fall of man when Adam and Eve had sinned against Him. God had always been looking for someone to enter into a covenant with so that He could bless, could be good to, and could show off His unmerited and undeserved favor. Our relationship and our inheritance are based on the covenant God made with Abraham. In Galatians 3:29, it says how we in Christ are Abraham's seed and an heir according to the promise. God's promise to Abraham can be found throughout the book of Genesis but also summed up in Romans 4:13 where it says, "For the promise, that he should be the heir of the world, was not to Abraham's, or to his seed, through the law (the law of Moses is what it's talking about i.e the famous Ten Commandments) but through the righteousness of faith." Are you getting it yet? Have you noticed a common theme in this journey of mine? Walking by faith and not by sight (2 Corinthians 5:7) and seeking HIS RIGHTEOUSNESS and not my own (Matthew 6:33) are my themes. This is something Abraham did very well, except for when he had a baby out of wedlock with Hagar the maid, and not his wife Sarah. Abraham and Sarah were trying to help God out with the promise He gave them that they would have a child, but Abraham was 100 years old and Sarah was 90 years old. If you read the entire story, that didn't stop God from blessing Abraham with what He promised Him, a child of their own.

How many times have we all failed and messed up, and God has still come through on His promises? It wasn't because of our works or because we were perfect; it was because of our faith. Whether it was Adam and

Eve, Abraham, Moses, Solomon, David, who saw a married woman, had sex with her then killed her husband as a cover-up to his sin, or Saul who later became Paul and wrote 2/3rd of the New Testament, all had sinned and fallen short of the glory of God. There was only one perfect man, and God said because I could swear by no greater, I will swear by myself (Hebrews 6:13) which is where Jesus came into the picture.

We don't deserve anything from God based on our own merit because of sin, but we can receive it freely as a gift through what Jesus did at the cross for us. I like to keep it simple and put it this way, we can live a "good life" based on what Jesus did for us. These are the things that I held on to while walking out this journey, and I still hold on and put them to practice today. I of course still fall short and mess up all the time, but it says in His Word that His grace is sufficient and His strength is made perfect in our weakness (2 Corinthians 12:9). Now, by no way am I saying just do all kind of wrong and bad things because that's not the true nature of God either; but what I am saying is if you receive and focus on Jesus, His finished work on the cross and His righteousness, not our own, you won't want to do all kinds of wrong and bad things. You will actually sin less not more. Romans 6:14 says, "Sin shall not have dominion over you for you're not under the law, but under grace." Grace is His unmerited, undeserved favor which I know without a doubt I have, and I believe this is why so many other doors have opened for me to share my story in the past year.

I'm typically an introvert and shy person by nature, never looking to draw attention to myself or even wanting or caring for anyone to notice me. It's even hard for me to approach a really nice-looking woman I might see and want to talk to, just to be really transparent. I still struggle in that area among other things to this day, but God has given me a true story to share. It has opened doors for me to share with a lot of people. It has even given me a desire to share my story with family and friends from Ohio to California and anywhere in between. I have been able to share at churches and even at bars. I have even been invited to do a local TV show, my first ever, in Long Beach with my friend and sister in Christ, Tyra, also know as T-Lily from the T-Lily Show along with many other speaking engagements that have taken place, both planned and unplanned. It's actually become easier for me to talk when it comes to the things of God because I'm always hearing Him say to me in my heart, "STEP OUT! Someone needs to hear this." He is always right; I can tell by the looks on people's faces and their responses. It's all very humbling to be used by God that He would love and think that much of me to use me, especially when I never thought much of myself. By reading His Word, I have found He thinks very highly of me, and He thinks the same about YOU also. We are the apple of His eye (Psalms 17:8). He also says we are heirs of God and joint-heirs with Christ (Romans 8:17), so we have a right to expect his goodness and favor not because of our works but because of our faith in Christ.

Anything that I've talked about in my testimony is to let you know God can and WILL do the same things for you if you just believe. If you believe right then, the right words will follow, and He will place His desires in your heart (Psalms 37:4). Even writing this book was a step of faith, like all of this, because I used to think, "Who would care to hear anything I have to say? I'm no one that special. I don't even want or like to talk," but that's not what God says about me or any of His children. I knew in my heart and without a doubt, this was what He wanted me to do. I've been doing a lot of things I've never done in the two-plus years I've lived in California, but I know it was a setup and all part of His plan, part of my relationship with Him as Father and me as His son. All part of His Amazing Grace!!

To anyone who wants to get to know Jesus Christ or has never accepted Him and entered into this covenant to receive the inheritance God has already set up for you, all you have to do is accept Him as Lord and savior. Just say, "Lord Jesus, I recognize I'm a sinner and in need of a Savior. Come into my life. I need you, help me, and be my Savior; and I will live for you the rest of my life. Thank you for saving me!!" It's really that simple.

2 Corinthians 5:17 says, "If any man be in Christ he is a new creature, old things are passed away and all

things become new." You are a new creation. Find a good local church or ministers who teach on the true nature of God, and get ready to receive your inheritance due to you not because of who you are but because of Whose you are. **<u>You are a child of God in Christ!</u>**

Acknowledgments

To my parents, **Robert and JoAnne Barnes,** thank you for being what parents should be and making it easy to honor you. Thank you for your prayers, for loving me unconditionally, and for bringing both a holy fear or reverence and faith into our relationship, which helped me grow into who I am as a man. I couldn't ask for better people to call my mom and dad. God has truly blessed me. Love you to life.

To my brothers, Lee Barnes and Robert Cauley, thank you for your support. I know we don't talk all the time; but I feel your love, prayers, and support as brothers. I appreciate you both more than you know, especially being there for the family as I moved out of state. Love you to life as well.

Special thanks to my Sister-In-Law Felicia Cauley, thank you for helping me with the process of writing my first ever book, and inspiring me to put it out there. I appreciate your knowledge and support, as I could not have done this without you. Love you, sis.

I want to lastly say a super, super huge **THANK YOU** to anyone and everyone who has had anything to do with being in this thing called life with me and inspiring me through this journey. Thank you to all of my family, friends, coworkers, acquaintances, and even just random people I've met from Ohio to California and anywhere in between. There are way too many names of people to thank, but just know God used you whether you realized it or not, especially the ones who came along at pivotal times in this journey along with writing this book. I would not be where I am today without you, your support, and your prayers. Also, many thanks to all of the churches, non-profit, and faith-based organizations that allowed me to exercise my faith and serve in the communities both in Ohio and California. My prayer for you is, may the Lord bless you and keep you. May His face shine on you and be gracious to you all!

About the Author

Troy Barnes lives in Lake Forest, California, and works as an IT professional spanning twenty years, ten as a certified IT asset management professional working for various companies. Troy is passionate about helping and serving others, as he has given his time and resources to various churches and organizations both in Ohio and California. He is continuously growing in his life journey seeking God's overall plan for his life. Troy stays active by working out, volunteering, and spending time with friends and family. *Amazing Grace* is his first-ever book. You can follow him on Facebook, LinkedIn as Troy Barnes, and Instagram as tbarnes2432; or you can email him at <u>tbarnes2432@gmail.com</u> .

CPSIA information can be obtained
at www.ICGtesting.com
Printed in the USA
FSHW021956081120
75729FS

9 780998 864495